Too Much Of A Good Thing:
Are You Addicted to Your Smartphone?

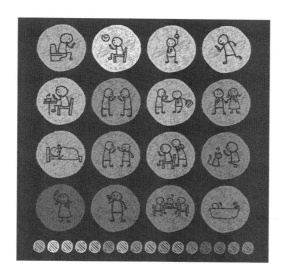

Dr. James A. Roberts
Sentia Publishing Company

Copyright© 2017 by Dr. James A. Roberts

Sentia Publishing Company has the exclusive rights to reproduce this work, to prepare derivative works from this work, to publicly distribute this work, to publicly perform this work, and to publicly display this work.

All rights reserved. No part of this publication may be reproduced, stored in a retrieval system, or transmitted, in any form or by any means, electronic, mechanical, photocopying, recording, or otherwise, without the prior written permission of the copyright owner.

ISBN: 978-1-5496063-1-1

Printed in the United States of America in Austin, Texas.

Contents

Author's Note 1
Bonus Chapter 3
Chapter 1 13
Chapter 2 21
Chapter 3 37
Chapter 4 63
Chapter 5 69
Chapter 6 79
Chapter 7 91
Chapter 8 103
Chapter 9 117
Chapter 10 127
Endnotes 141

About the Author

JAMES A. ROBERTS is a well-known author with approximately 100 articles published in the academic literature. He is currently the Ben H. Williams Professor of Marketing at Baylor University in Waco, Texas where he has been a faculty member since 1991. Too Much of a Good Thing (his second book) follows closely on the heels of his highly successful first book, Shiny Objects, which focused its attention on how our love of money and material possessions impacts our happiness.

Dr. Roberts is a nationally recognized expert on human/consumer behavior and has studied one form or another of addictive behavior for the past 15 years. He has been quoted extensively in the media and has appeared on the CBS Early Show, ABC World News Tonight, NBC's The Today Show, Yahoo. com's "The Daily Ticker," and has been quoted or featured on The O'Reilly Factor, US News & World Report, The New York Times, USA Today, The Wall Street Journal, National Public Radio, Cosmopolitan Magazine, Yahoo! Tech (one million page views), and countless other newspapers, magazines, websites, and television appearances.

About The Book

With his current effort, Dr. Roberts asks readers if they may be getting "Too Much of a Good Thing" regarding their smartphone use. This is no hoity-toity treatise but a fun and humorous look at our attachment (addiction?) to our smartphones. In chapter two you can respond to 12 short statements and see for yourself. Are you addicted to your smartphone? And, if you are, "What's the big deal?" In Chapter Three, experts tell us whether we can actually be addicted to our smartphones. The act of phubbing (phone snubbing) and its impact on your relationships is broached in chapters 4-6.

But the fun doesn't stop there. Chapter Seven offers a crash course on smartphone etiquette while chapter eight shares some interesting (and often sobering) facts about driving while distracted. Chapter Nine debunks the four myths about multi-tasking and how our phones may undermine our productivity at school and work. Finally, he offers some easy solutions to all this telephony. SmartPhone Smack Down is all about carving out some time away from your smartphone so you can explore all the wonders available off-line if you just take a few minutes to power down. This is a life-changing book and a journey that Dr. Roberts looks forward to sharing with you. So, put your smartphone on "airplane mode" and let's get started.

Author's Note

Bonus chapter! Already a classic, the 2017 updated edition of "Smartphone Love affair" contains a new chapter on our Commander-in-Chief's Twitter habits. Is president Donald J. Trump addicted to Twitter? Are you addicted to Twitter? Read this exciting "Bonus Chapter" to find out.

Thanks for considering reading my book—it's a real lifechanger. Before you read any further I wanted to make one thing abundantly clear: I love technology. I can still remember the days when I would have to wait 2-3 weeks to get a copy of an article or information on somebody or something. Now, with the click of a few buttons I have what I need or want. This instant access to information and entertainment still amazes me and is much appreciated.

I have also had a Facebook page for around 10 years, blog, have a Twitter account that I use when I have something to say, and I text often enough. But, to be totally honest, I have yet to "pin" anything or post a picture to Instagram. This is not, however, so uncommon for a male. Pinterest visitors are largely female (71%) and Instagram has more female visitors than males (56% vs. 44%).

So, this book is by no means anti-technology. I however, like many of you, can hear a faint voice (nearly drowned out by our constant state of distraction) that's saying, "I really love my smartphone, but maybe it's time I cut back a bit on how much I use it." Like the title of this book, we may be getting too much of a good thing. This book is all about helping you find your "digital sweet spot."

That's the place where you are making full use of all that your smartphone and other technologies have to offer AND carving out time for offline activities that nurture your soul, allow you to spend uninterrupted time with friends and family, maybe get some work done, and plug into larger important causes like politics, religion or what have you.

This book was written with the modern reader in mind. It should only take two hours to read and a little longer if you spend a few minutes to take the cell phone addiction and phubbing scales which I highly recommend. Can someone really be addicted to their smartphone? And, what's phubbing? Both excellent questions but you will have to read the book to find out. I wrote this book in a conversational style with a good bit of humor and a lot of fun facts to boot.

Did you know that the human attention span is now 8.25 seconds compared to nine seconds for the standard issue Goldfish? Really, we can't focus as long as "Goldie" our pet goldfish? Find out why inside these covers. So, happy reading and don't hesitate to text, tweet, post, or e-mail (just not while you're driving) if you have any comments or questions for me. I would love to hear from you.

Happy Reading,
Jim

BONUS CHAPTER

Tweet Like Trump:

A lot has been made about President Donald J. Trump's Twitter "habit." At first blush it appears that our "Twitter in Chief" can't control his tweeting.

He's not the only one. There are 67 million Twitter users in the US alone. Twitter acolytes around the world send out an amazing 6,000 tweets every second, 350,000 tweets per minute, 500 million tweets per day and 200 billion tweets every year. No tweets, however, garner the attention paid to those that emanate from @realDonaldTrump or @POTUS. Is DJT a Twitter addict or is he sly like a fox?

This chapter has a two-fold purpose. First, I take a brief look at @Potus' Twitter habits and attempt to determine (using my very own Twitter Addiction Scale) if our Twitter-in-Chief may be addicted to tweeting. Second, I provide the same Twitter Addiction Scale for you to assess your own tweeting habits. It's possible that both our Twitter-in-Chief and many of us are Twitter addicts. And, if you don't use Twitter (25% of us do), don't be too smug. The remainder of this scintillating book explores our obsession with smartphones and what it means for our personal happiness, the quality of our relationships, and our productivity at work. There's even a smartphone addiction scale you can take in Chapter 3.

But, first things first. Is Donald J. Trump addicted to tweeting? Addiction, you might say, is a strong word. Addiction, whether it's to drugs, alcohol, exercise, sex or social media is best understood as "continuing a behavior despite its negative consequences for you and others around you". And, yes, we can be addicted to behaviors like tweeting just like we can be addicted to drugs or alcohol. Anything that produces pleasure in our brains can lead to addiction.

Harvard researchers found that we get a real "buzz" (the reward centers of our brains light up like Christmas trees) when we share with others. And that's really what Twitter is all about - sharing information and your opinions with others. A prominent psychologist (Paul Atchley of Kansas University) states that our smartphones are nothing more than "drug-delivery systems". Our brains get a rush of dopamine (feeling of euphoria) from sharing personal information with others. Access to e-mail, texting and social media provide a 24-7 conduit for telling the world what we think about our new Commander-in-Chief or about the 83 sparkling-clean bathrooms at the 68,000 square foot Bucee's convenience store on Interstate 35 near New Braunfels, Texas.

So, is President Trump a Twitter addict? What follows is a Twitter addiction scale that I developed for this very purpose. The scale is based on the six core components of any addiction: salience, euphoria, tolerance, withdrawal symptoms, conflict, and relapse. These are the six signs medical professionals check for when deciding whether you're a bit too in love with the grape or have an unhealthy attachment to your Twitter account.

Based upon my 20 plus years of research in the area of behavioral addictions (shopping and smartphones), what follows is my assessment of DJT's attachment to Twitter. It's not the same as having the Donald himself take the quiz, but I am confident it paints a pretty accurate picture of Trump's Twitter tendencies.

Create a mental picture of me sitting across from President Trump in the Blue room of the White House (ala Jake Taper's recent interview). He's had a long day at the office, but has graciously consented to answer my twelve questions as it relates to his Twitter use. The questions I "asked" appear below with my bold-facing of @Potus' response to each question.

Is Donald Trump addicted to Twitter?

Twitter Addiction Scale

I. **Salience**
   1. I send tweets throughout the day.
      YES
      NO
   2. I feel compelled to tweet my opinions on topics important to me.
      YES
      NO

II. **Euphoria**:
   1. I feel great when my tweets get a lot of attention.
      YES
      NO
   2. I feel better after tweeting something that needs to be said.
      YES
      NO

III. **Tolerance**
   1. Recently, I find myself tweeting more and more.
      YES
      NO
   2. I spend more time tweeting than I should.
      YES
      NO

IV. **Withdrawal Symptom**
   1. I get anxious when I can't tweet out my thoughts on something.
      YES
      NO
   2. I would go into a panic if I lost access to my Twitter account.
      YES
      NO

V. **Conflict**
   1. I have had serious arguments with others over my tweeting.
      YES
      NO
   2. My romantic partner says I need to cut back on my tweeting.
      YES
      NO

VI. **Release**
   1. I have tried to cut back on my tweeting but could not.
      YES
      NO
   2. I have tried to be more civil when tweeting but always
      go back to name calling and negative comments.
      YES
      NO

Donald J. Trump's Twitter Addiction Score: ___10___

Your Twitter addiction score: _____

Results Key:

8+ "Yes" answers

> You need a Twitter intervention if you can find any friends or family still speaking to you. Alternatively, I can personally make a reservation for you at the Kim Kardashian Clinic for Social Media Addiction. I see anger management classes in your future.

5-7 "Yes" answers

> You are at a crossroads regarding your Twitter use. It's time to set limits on your twitter use before you have no friends left.

3-4 "Yes" answers

> You are in pretty good shape, at least in regard to your tweeting, but must remain ever vigilant or it could be the start of the slippery slope to Twitter Hell.

0-2 "Yes" answers

> You either don't use Twitter or have the self-control of a Zen master. Keep up the good work and you can cross "Twitter Addict" off your list of bad social media habits.

As my channeling of Donald Trump suggests, our Commander-in-Chief is strongly attached, dare I say addicted, to tweeting. Or, more colloquially, he has an itchy Twitter finger. Let's take a closer look at his results.

Salience. President Trump gets one of his only two "NO"s in this category. His tendency to send most tweets late at night or early in the morning earns him one of his two "negative" results. The second question in this category is an easy yes. The Donald appears to feel compelled to sound off on subjects that vary from building a wall between the US and Mexico to Rosie O'Donnell's weight and sexual orientation.

Euphoria: Donald loves attention and no doubt gets a rush when he stirs the pot with an incendiary tweet. Another "Yes" for question one of this section. President Trump loves to hold court and no doubt gets a rush of dopamine when he shares with his 30 million plus Twitter followers.

Tolerance: Donald's tweeting does not appear to have abated despite his suggestions that he might cut back on his tweeting once he secured the presidency. This, however, is really better discussed later when talking about relapse as a sign of addiction. Donald's second "NO" comes in this category. It appears that he has shifted some of his tweeting responsibilities to white house staffers. In fact, analysis suggests that his tweets from @Potus are often more kind hearted than the tweets that emanate from his personal Twitter handle @realDonaldTrump. It is likely that the responsibilities of the most powerful office on the earth has forced President Trump to outsource the more perfunctory tweets that need to be sent.

Withdrawal Symptoms: Clearly, Donald cannot resist the urge to express his thoughts to his many Twitter followers. A solid "Yes" for the first question of this section. I am not sure that President Trump can imagine losing access to his beloved Twitter. I would love to hear personally from him on this question.

Conflict: I am not sure whether this even needs to be discussed. Think of the combative back and forth with Rosie O'Donnell, parents of deceased Iraqi War Veteran Army captain Humayun Khan, and Alicia Machado the disgruntled 1996 Miss Universe pageant winner. A big fat "No" on Question one of this category. I admit I am going out on the limb on the second question, but I am comfortable in arguing that Melania would like to be able to take back many of the things her romantic-partner-in-chief has shared on Twitter.

Relapse: At one point in his campaign, President Trump hinted that he would probably cut back on his tweeting once he was elected. So far, this is one campaign "promise" he has not kept. @realDonaldTrump's tweets continue to be hyperbolic and disagreeable (condescending?). This earns him a final "No" on the last question of my Twitter addiction scale.

As the "Results Key" suggests, our current Twitter-in-Chief has an unhealthy attachment to his Twitter account. He is in full-blown addiction and is in desperate need of a Twitter intervention. Imagine Melania, Baron, Ivanka, Tiffany, Donald Jr. and Eric (possibly his spiritual advisor Paula White?) sitting in the "War Room" under the White House with an intervention specialist (see "Intervention", the TV show). They are waiting for the President-in-Chief to walk through the door under the false pretense that they had new evidence about the real head count at his inauguration.

These interventions are tricky things. At first, there is the usual denial but after one sob story after another, the accused at least makes a half-hearted nod toward changing his ways. But, like most addictions, Twitter addiction will likely not go away without a fight and multiple relapses. In this imaginary scenario, I don't see @Potus' tweeting ever going away but possibly morphing into a kinder, gentler version of his current tweets, in the years ahead.

Why does Trump's Twitter addiction matter?

So, why you might ask, 'Do we care if our Commander-In-Chief is a Twitter addict? We could talk about how such an addiction could be damaging to President Trump and his many personal relationships (read chapter seven of this book for more on that), but that's not what has most of us really worried. It's the position Trump holds and the unfettered and expansive platform afforded through his Twitter account that has us up at night. And, this is not just me. A recent Wall Street Journal/NBC News poll found that a broad swath of American adults think The Donald should cut back on his tweeting.

As a form of computer-mediated-communication (CMC), Twitter suffers (like all social media) from the information lost by such media. Lost is our ability to detect sarcasm, tone of voice, facial expressions, and body language. Research has found that in face-to-face interactions up to 10,000 nonverbal cues are exchanged in the first minute alone. In addition to the lack of cues needed to decipher others' thoughts, social media encourages unfiltered musings, incomplete thoughts that can be damaging.

For most of us, I have 55 twitter followers, these incomplete thoughts are lost and quickly forgotten in the sea of tweets that go out every day. When you are the President of the United States, the stakes are much higher. In addition to the 30 million plus Twitter followers of Donald Trump, the media (and political opponents, no doubt) are just waiting to pounce on every tweet that goes out under @POTUS or @realDonaldTrump. The Donald's tweets do make a difference. An ill-conceived idea by House Republicans to abolish the independent Senate Ethics Committee was quickly derailed by a few tweets from the Twitter-in-Chief.

Score one for the big guy. In fact, the South Korean government has a "Twitter watching" team assigned to analyze Trump's tweets. Anyone with access and the codes to the Nuclear Football should take a measured approach to what they say. Donald Trump has obtained the positional authority he so craved. My prayer is that he will gain the spiritual authority that is needed to make good, moral, and reasoned decisions given that so much of the global community's well-being hangs in the balance.

Et Tu?

Now that we have bared the president's soul in regard to his tweeting, it's time to turn the spotlight on you. If you are a twitter user, 67 million of us are, take the Twitter addiction scale above and see how you do. If you are not a Twitter user you are by no means off the hook. Turn to chapter three of this book and take the smartphone addiction scale. My years of research experience on the topic of smartphone addiction, and my many observations on the pain and suffering (physical and mental) associated with unhealthy smartphone use, suggest that addiction to technology of any sort can have disastrous results for your personal happiness, relationships, and productivity at work or school. So, read on as if your life depends on it - because it does.

Chapter 1

Cellularitis:

A Socially Transmitted Disease (STD) that results in habitual use of one's cell phone to the detriment of his or her psychological and physical health and well-being.

Used with permission by King Features Syndicate

I call it cellularitis. Like the common cold, it spreads from human to human. But, unlike Nasopharyngitis (the common cold), no one has to sneeze on you to catch cellularitis. And, this STD (Socially Transmitted Disease) is highly contagious. The simple act of being in close proximity to someone using their smartphone causes us to search for solace in our own cellular pacifier.

Similar to anthropologists who study primates in their natural setting, two intrepid University of Michigan researchers studied the cell phone habits of the possibly wildest primate of them all—teens and young adults.[1] The pair positioned themselves near restaurants and coffee shops in and around the University of Michigan campus. Over four months they observed the communication rituals of teens and young adults as they ate lunch or sipped their espresso. They recorded cell phone use in 10-second increments in these "public dyads" (two people in public) for up to 20 minutes. What they found was that people were twice as likely to pull out their cell phone if their companion did so. And, here's the big finish, women were more likely than men to do so whether talking to other women or men.

Two reasons were given why this might be the case: (1) prompting and (2) exclusion. Prompting suggests that when we see somebody checking their phone or taking a call or text, we are reminded that we may have an "urgent" matter that needs to be taken care of as well. Personally, I think social exclusion might be a better explanation for such behavior. Old manners die hard. Even in our technology obsessed culture, it is still seen as rude or off-putting for someone to abandon a conversation in mid-stream to attend to other matters.

So, to avoid being socially excluded, we whip out our cell phone and check the "likes" to our last post on Instagram or update our Facebook status. Women were the worst offenders because social inclusion is more important to them. Additionally, women are more attached than men to their cell phones. A recent survey I did with college students found that women were more attached (addicted) to their cell phones, and used them an astounding 10 hours per day compared to a relatively paltry seven and a half hours per day for male college students.

Is cell phone use merely contagious (like a cold), something we catch then simply get over it? Or, could our current preoccupation with our cell phones be something more sinister? Could we actually be addicted to our cell phones?

Addiction has been defined in many ways over the years but usually involves the repeated use of a substance despite the negative consequences suffered by the addicted individual. In the last 20 years or so, however, our understanding of what it means to be addicted has expanded to encompass behaviors including sex, gambling, exercise, eating, Internet and cell phone use to name a few. The medical and mental health communities now believe that any entity that can produce a pleasurable sensation has the potential of becoming addictive. A behavioral addiction, just like a substance addiction, is a powerful drive to continue a particular behavior despite the negative consequences for the individual and those around him. It's all really very medical. Any behavior that we repeat frequently can spark a cascade of biochemical processes with the release of the neurotransmitter dopamine (good stuff) which produces a sense of excitment and well-being in the pleasure centers of our brain.[2] We get a "buzz," so to speak, from performing the behavior.

Your Brain's Pleasure Centers

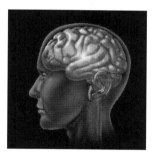

Nucleus Accumbens

Ventral Tegmental Area (VTA)

Prefontal Cortex

Amygdala

Hypothalmus

Septum

The loss of control over the behavior in question, let's say habitual cell phone use, is a sure sign that you may be addicted to your cellular device—similar to free-basing cocaine or taking a hit from a crack pipe. For example, you may have had an accident or several close calls while talking/texting while driving but you still continue to use your cell phone while driving. Or, a common occurrence for a college professor like me is the student who repeatedly uses his or her cell phone in class despite repeated warnings and penalties for such behavior.

I hate to be the bearer of bad news parents, but it's likely that Camille or Chloe' spend more time checking their Facebook status than they do paying attention to my engrossing lectures. Granted, their cell phone may be a lot more interesting than my talk on the nuances of outdoor advertising, but with the cost of a private college education reaching and surpassing $50,000 per year at many institutions of higher learning it is very likely not in the best interest of their (or yours!) financial future.

Americans have had a long-held fascination, many argue obsession, with technology. Our modern fascination with technology began with the radio in the 1920s and 1930s. Next, it was the telephone. I love early ads for the telephone that had to argue its merits to a skeptical public. It was TV, however, that nearly put an end to any type of human interaction. Even with all of the distractions available today, the average American still logs a solid five hours per day in front of the old boob tube.

The mid 90s witnessed the emergence of the Internet, the first new communication medium since the TV. The Internet quickly spread throughout the world dramatically altering how we communicate with our fellow man.

This fascination with technology continues to run rampant in the 21st century as the time U.S. consumers spend with technology continues to escalate.[3] The current obsession with the cell phone is simply an extension of a 100-year trend of people from all walks of life spending more time with technology and less with fellow humans.[4] At present, there are more than 325 million cell phones in the US with a population of approximately 311 million people.[5] Did you know that Americans toss out 140 million, yes that's millions, of cell phones every year?[6] Where, you might ask, do all these unwanted phones end up? It's actually quite a sordid tale and is the subject of a later chapter in this book.

Cell phones have become an integral part of who we are—extensions of our self. An appendage of sorts, that when cut off, leads to disastrous results. Most of us cannot conceive of life without our cell phone. In an earlier paper I published with co-author and friend Chris Manolis of Xavier University, I refer to our dependence on cell phones as an "invisible addiction." They have become so integrated into our lives that we don't realize how dependent/addicted we have become to our cell phones.

Our smartphones are our link to others, helping us to maintain and nurture social relationships as well as conducting the more mundane exigencies of our everyday lives.[7]

Research tells us that the average American can't leave his or her cell phone alone for more than 6.5 minutes checking them up to a 150 times every day.[8] Do you consider yourself a Facebook fanatic? Unless you're visiting the social networking site a minimum of 14 times per day you are below the national average. It will take 30 minutes of Facebook time, via your cell phone to keep up with average cellular Facebook denizen.[9]

Clearly, the culprit in all this is the modern smartphone. Well over half of all cell phone users own a smartphone and over 2/3 of 18-24 year olds own one. Smartphones are quickly eclipsing laptops and desktops as the preferred means of accessing the Internet. Fifty-six percent of Internet users access the Web via their cell phones. This figure has doubled from only a few years ago.[10] Cell phones have the dual advantage of both portability and accessibility. They are easy to carry with us and are always available (with the exception of low batteries and "out-of-area" warnings).

Smartphones have placed computers at the fingertips of nearly every American including our oldest (it may be the "not-so-smart" Jitterbug) and youngest—electronic pacifiers. Is there a need for anything else? We can make a call (increasingly passé), send a text, take a picture, play music, navigate our way, set a personal best on Angry Birds, surf the Web, go shopping, place a bid on eBay, or keep track of our finances, make a bank deposit, and remind ourselves of important events (birthdays, meetings, holidays, etc.). This ever-expanding array of cell phone functions has made their use even more prone to over-use and even addiction. We are the most wired generation in history.[11]

Our current cell phone use is a solid example of what I refer to as a Paradox of technology.[12] We can't live without them but we also can't live with them. Smartphones can be both freeing and enslaving at the same time. The smartphone allows us to stay in touch with family, friends, colleagues, and even strangers, gather endless amounts of data (if you're on an unlimited plan) and continue to live our lives without the restrictions of being tied to a particular location. At the same time, however, cell phones can be enslaving and lead to dependence and more restrictions. Take my older brother John, for example. He was very excited to get a coveted Blackberry years ago when he began his job as assistant council to a large company until he quickly learned that this meant that his boss could, and did, contact him at all hours of the day. Being available 24-7 is no one's idea of a good time.

Has our increasing reliance on the wondrous cell phones morphed into something more than simply a habit but possibly an addiction? Chapter two tackles this very issue. Do you display any (or all) of the six warning signs of cell phone addiction? I bet you already have a hunch but let's put your cell phone use to the test.

Food for Thought

Have you caught Cellularitis? Why or why not?
1. What do you like most about your smartphone?
2. What do you like least about your smartphone?
3. What activities do you spend the most time doing on your smartphone?
4. What would you like your smartphone to do that it currently cannot?

Chapter 2

The Six Signs of Cell Phone Addiction

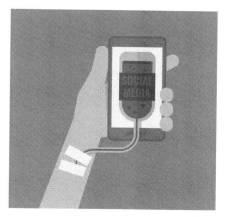

"My Cell phone is My Best Friend. It's My Lifeline to the Outside World."

— *Carrie Underwood*

Carrie Underwood, American Idol winner and successful singer/entertainer, is by no means alone in her attachment to her cell phone. U.S. teens and young adults can no longer envision a life without cell phones. In a large survey of teens, 47% said their social life would be considerably worse without their cell phone.[13] Second only to clothes, these same teens say their cell phones tell the most about their social status. And, they text a lot, much more than they talk! The average teen sends 3,200 text messages each month. And that's just the average. Stories of 10,000 or more texts a month are common from exasperated parents of teens.

Approximately half of all teens, in the flood of hormones that characterizes teenage life, exclaimed their social life would end if they couldn't text or access social media. Roughly the same percentage say they can text blindfolded,[14] and I've seen it —

under the desktop, or in their purse or back-pack, or even in their pocket. I have a friend who is a dentist who communicated that many teens text when they're in the dental chair. A recent survey I conducted with Xavier University colleague Chris Manolis, found that the average college student spends 8 hours and 48 minutes on their cell phone in a typical day. Females spend an average of ten hours per day on their phones and men about 7.5 hours each day.[15] Most Americans (teens, young adults, and older adults) can't leave their cell phone alone for more than six and a half minutes checking them up to 150 times per day.[16]

So, do you have the attention span of a Goldfish? If you do, you are a bit ahead of the curve. A study by computer giant Microsoft recently found that the average attention span of Homo Sapiens is 8.25 seconds—lagging behind the nine second attention span of Carassius Auratus (the common Goldfish). How they measured the attention span of a Goldfish I have no idea.

Our 140 character conversations, flood of brief texts populated with emojis and rapidly vanishing Snap Chats has reduced our attention spans from 12 seconds in 2000 to 8.25 seconds in 2015. A recent study found that a typical person shifts his or her attention between their smartphone, laptop, and other tech devices 21 times each hour. The typical office worker (me included) checks their e-mail approximately 30 times every hour. It's no surprise we never get any work done.[17]

One does not, however, begin life as a cell phone addict— it's a process. The process of addiction begins when a normally innocent behavior (shopping, plastic surgery, Internet use, exercise, cell phone use) turns damaging and slowly mutates into an addiction.[18] This "pre-addiction process" begins when an otherwise benign behavior with little or no harmful consequences (e.g., owning a cell phone for safety purposes) begins to evoke negative consequences as the user becomes increasingly dependent upon its use.

As the original purpose behind the purchase of a cell phone is buried under mountains of text messages, hours on Facebook, Instagram, and Pinterest, YouTube videos, and Words with Friends negative consequences begin to emerge. It might be lower productivity at work or school because of the intrusion of the cell phone on work or study time, arguments with friends and family members over your cell phone use, or increasingly more dangerous behaviors such as texting or talking while driving. All behavioral addictions eventually reach a "tipping point" where the affected individual can no longer control their cell phone use and the quality, and even quantity (in the case of texting and driving) of their lives are being undermined.

This burgeoning addiction leads to a disconnect between the processes of "liking" and "wanting." This shift from liking something to wanting or needing it is referred to as the "inflection point."[19] This tipping or inflection point marks a transition from a formerly harmless behavior that may have been pleasurable (staying up late to play Angry Birds on your phone) with few harmful consequences into an addictive behavior where want (mind and/or body) has replaced liking as the motivation behind the behavior. The precise biochemical processes that are launched by the ingestion of illicit substances also occurs when pleasurable behaviors are performed.[20]

Early detection of behavioral addictions is essential. Once you have crossed the line from "liking" to "wanting" (your tipping point) treatment becomes considerably more difficult. The earlier you detect a problem, the easier it is to treat. Even with early detection beating behavioral addictions can be difficult. An addiction to one's cell phone may also signal other behavioral or substance addictions. When one addiction exists the likelihood of others hiding in the shadows increases. And, often when one addiction is addressed others may pop up to take its place. For example, treatment may help a person disengage from dependence on their cell phone but this behavior might be replaced with other technology or behavioral addictions or even a substance addiction. It is critical to successful treatment of cell phone addiction to understand the rewards one receives from its over use.

It may be that addiction to one's cell phone is a "secondary addiction" where one's use of the cell phone is to escape an underlying problem (low self-esteem, boredom, impulsiveness, interpersonal problems). There is even a theory to explain such behavior—Escape Theory. When your current situation is so painful, for any of the reasons above or a whole host of problems not listed, you attempt to escape these negative events or feelings by busying yourself with other tasks. It's a little like sweeping your problems under the rug. They're still there but temporarily out of sight and mind while you activate your escape plan.

Cell phones may be used to avoid awkward social situations, connect with others, fight off boredom, or forget about your failing career or recent rocky relationship (you can fill in the blank with any of the myriad negative events we as humans must cope with). A focus on the "here and now" helps avoid reflecting on one's troubles. The problem is, however, that such distractions are not an effective coping strategy. At the end of the day, the problem is still there and new problems created from your addictive behavior are added to the mix.

So, it's come down to this. Have you reached your "tipping point" when it comes to your cell phone use? Fortunately, we have identified what is considered the six core components of any type of addiction—substance or behavioral.[21] I call them the six signs of cell phone addiction. They include: salience, mood modification, tolerance, withdrawal, conflict, and relapse. Please read my description of these six signs that follow and answer each of the two questions at the end of each description. By the time you've completed this task we will have a better idea of whether you've reached your "tipping point" when it comes to your cell phone use.

The Six Signs of Cell Phone Addiction Scale

1. **Salience**—a behavior becomes salient when it is deeply integrated into your daily routine. It is an essential activity that dominates your thinking, dictates your emotions, and plays an important role, in your daily routine. A Harris Interactive poll shows that a third of us check our cell phones during movies. Twenty percent do this during church. Nearly 10 percent have admitted to checking their phones during intimate moments. Some take selfies with the dearly departed at funerals. And a new trend of taking a selfie while on the toilet— aka, the "poopie"— has emerged.

    Sixty-eight percent of adult Americans sleep with their cell phone next to their bed.[22] And, this is causing problems for many whose sleep is being interrupted throughout the night by tweets (not from the birds outside), beeps, vibrations, bells, and whistles that are part of your cell phone's irresistibility. In essence, your phone is saying, "You can't ignore me, I am essential to your happiness and I won't be ignored." The light from your nighttime cell phone use can interrupt your circadian rhythms and block the production of melatonin that is essential for a good night's sleep. Only 29 percent of people turn their cell phone off at night. Are you one of the many U.S. adults who check your cell phones up to 150 times a day?[23]

Even if your cell phone is interrupting a good night's sleep, it doesn't end there. Seventy-nine percent of 18-44 year olds reach for their cell phone within 15 minutes of waking. Fifty-four percent of 18-24 year olds use their cell phone as an alarm clock. So, if your cell phone is the first thing you reach for in the morning and the last thing you see at night, and it's your bedside companion throughout the night, you may have reached your "tipping point." Sixty-three percent of cell phone owners keep their phones by their side for all but an hour or two of their day.[24]

How many texts do you send each day? About 50 is average for the typical user. E-mails? Tweets? Facebook? Instagram? Pinterest (for you ladies)? Sports? Weather? GPS? News? YouTube? Even while driving? A majority of people do. Texting, you bet. Do you take or make calls, or send texts while in the bathroom—nearly 40 percent do.[25] And, even maybe a few calls (very passé)? You get the picture (you probably took it on your cell phone). Your cell phone didn't take over your life overnight but slowly and quietly it has taken center stage in your daily activities. Research has shown that the longer we own our cell phone the more uses we find for it.

Answer the following two questions as it pertains to how salient your cell phone is to your everyday activities.

Is the first thing you reach for after waking in the morning your smartphone?
A. ☐Yes ☐No

Do you sleep with your smartphone next to your bed?
B. ☐Yes ☐No

2. **Euphoria (mood modification)**—is the feeling of anticipation or excitement that precedes and/or follows the use of your cell phone. Or, have you used your cell phone to avoid an awkward situation? Have you ever practiced "phonication" where you pretend to take a call to avoid talking to someone or to assuage feeling uncomfortable when you're standing alone in a social gathering? Who knows what the beep, buzz, whistle or stylized ring-tone might have in store for you—exciting stuff.

An uplifting text from a friend, a funny tweet, or hilarious six-second Vine video, or a racy disappearing Snapchat picture, or a large number of "likes" to various posts on Instagram, Pinterest, or Facebook can all brighten your day. Although not a very good coping strategy, a "phantom" call or urgent need to check one's phone have become an increasingly common way to cope with uncomfortable social situations. The cell phone is the cellular-pacifier for adults in the 21st century. Please answer the following two questions that ask the role your cell phone plays in managing your mood.

I often use my cell phone when I am bored.
A. ☐Yes ☐No

I have pretended to take calls to avoid awkward social situations.
B. ☐Yes ☐No

3. **Tolerance**—like in drug and alcohol abuse, addresses the need for an ever-increasing "dose" of the behavior to achieve the desired "high." Research has shown that the longer someone has had their cell phone the more they are likely to use it.[26] The increasing array of functions that can be performed on one's cell phone guarantees that our dependence on our cell phone is likely to increase. Please answer the following two questions as they relate to your cell phone use.

   I find myself spending more and more time on my cell phone.
   A. ☐Yes ☐No

   I spend more time than I should on my cell phone.
   B. ☐Yes ☐No

4. **Withdrawal symptoms**—The feelings of irritability, stress, anxiousness, desperation, and even panic that often occur when you are separated from your cell phone are good examples of withdrawal symptoms. I have seen all these reactions and more whenever my wife or daughters have misplaced their iPhones. Sixty-eight percent of all adults have an irrational fear of losing their phone. Younger adults are even more dependent on their phones—77 percent felt anxious when separated from their cell phones for even a few minutes.

British researchers first coined the term "nomophobia" (fear of no mobile phone) to describe the fear many of us feel when our cellular umbilical cord is severed for even the briefest of time.[27] How long was it before you replaced your cell phone the last time you broke it, lost it, or heaven forbid, had it stolen? My guess is not long—the same day if possible. These are the same types of reactions drug users have when separated from their drug of choice

An experiment conducted at the University of Maryland found that, "most college students are not just unwilling, but functionally unable to exist without media links to the world."[28] Subjects were asked to give up all media, including their cell phones, for 24 hours. How hard can that be? From the looks of it, very difficult to nearly impossible for most members of the cell phone brotherhood. One student quipped that she was, "addicted and the dependency is sickening." Numerous students reported that they started off their 24 hours unplugged feeling good, but noticed by lunch time that their mood started to change.

A creeping sense of isolation and loneliness started to dominate their thinking. By early afternoon an increasing sense of panic had set in. I may be missing important texts or calls, or updates, or other important events—this is not good. Then the fidgeting and irritability, that are also withdrawal symptoms for substance abusers, took over. The subjects' dependence on their cell phones and other media had actually caused physical symptoms of withdrawal. One student even commented that he felt "phantom vibrations" throughout the day.

Answer the following two questions as they relate to any type of withdrawal symptoms you may have experienced when separated from your cell phone.

I become agitated or irritable when my cell phone is out of sight.
A. ☐Yes ☐No

I have gone into a panic when I thought I had lost my cell phone.
B. ☐Yes ☐No

5. **Conflict**—is a common outcome from addiction to one's cell phone. It might be arguing about overages with your children or spouse, the number of texts your kids send (my daughter's high water mark was 8,500 for one month) or their mental absence at meals or car drives when they are plugged in. We have all been the victims of conversations when the other person has one eye on you and the other on his/her cell phone.

   My favorite attempt to avoid the inevitable conflict that comes with incessant cell phone use is what many college students do when they are in a group outing, let's say for dinner. They all place their cell phones in the middle of the table and whoever breaks down first to get their cell phone has to pay for dinner. Of course, what happens most of the time is that no such pact is agreed upon and you have various dinner partyers talking to those present, those not, or checking their phones for other urgent information.

   Have you ever been chastised for using your cell phone in a business meeting or when talking to your spouse or friend? Even children are complaining that they can't get their parent's attention because of constant cell phone use. Their solution: buy their child a cell phone—a simple solution, disastrous results. I can't tell you the number of times I have had to warn or levy penalties for habitual cell phone use during class.

Cell phones also interrupt our productivity at work or our ability to concentrate on our studies. And, don't even get me started on calling and/or texting while driving and the havoc that wreaks, that will be fodder for a later chapter's discussion. Please answer the following two questions as they relate to the conflict created in your life by your cell phone use.

I have argued with my spouse, friends, or family about my cell phone use.
A. ☐Yes ☐No
I use my cell phone while driving my car.
B. ☐Yes ☐No

6. **Relapse**—occurs when we acknowledge that our cell phone use may be undermining our well-being but when we attempt to stop we can't. It's like any bad habit we might have, say smoking or eating too much, we start a diet, attempt to quit smoking or drinking, only to relapse after a short period of time. I have been attempting to lose the same five pounds for twenty years. Have you ever attempted to go cold-turkey over phone use during family gatherings only to revert to the same old behavior after a few days?

It's like being an alcoholic; you must be constantly vigilant if you want to keep cell phones from invading every aspect of your life. Have you ever been interrupted by a text or phone call that you just had to answer when in the heat of the moment with your significant other? If you have, you may have crossed the tipping point. Please answer the following two questions as it relates to your attempts to control your cell phone use.

I have tried to cut-back on my cell phone use but it didn't last very long.
A. ☐Yes ☐No
I need to reduce my cell phone use but am afraid I can't do it.
B. ☐Yes ☐No

Your Cell Phone Addiction Score

Well, it's time to see if you have crossed the tipping point from reasonable cell phone use to potentially addictive cell phone habits. To calculate your score, simply add up the number of "Yes" responses to each of the twelve questions of my Six Signs of Cell phone Addiction scale.

Results Key:

8+ "Yes" answers: I will personally make a reservation for you at the Betty Ford Clinic for habitual cell phone users.

5-7 "Yes" answers: You have crossed the "tipping point" and are moving full-steam ahead to full-blown cell phone addiction.

3-4 "Yes" answers: You have not yet reached your "tipping point" but need to carefully assess how your cell phone is impacting your life.

0-2 "Yes" answers: You are either living in a monastery or at least have the patience and self-restraint of a monk. Or, technology simply scares you.

Author's Note

In early 2015 the above scale was posted on Yahoo!Tech and garnered nearly one million page views. Of the over 40,000 people who completed the scale, 26 % had 8+ "Yes" answers, 29% had 5-7 "Yes" answers, 25% had 3-4 "Yes" answers and 21% had 0-2 "Yes" answers.

In the next chapter I have assembled a panel of psychiatrists, psychologists, and MDs to answer four questions. Most importantly I ask these experts whether someone can be addicted to their smartphone. I also ask what they feel is the best thing someone can do to reduce their reliance on their smartphone. Read on. I think you will find what these experts have to say to be both very interesting and useful.

Food for Thought

1. Are you addicted to your smartphone? Why or why not?
2. Is your romantic partner addicted to their smartphone?
3. Do you agree that the six signs of cell phone addiction are good indicators of your dependence on your smartphone? Why or why not?
4. Do you use your smartphone in bed?
5. Do you think you could benefit from cutting back on your time on your smartphone? How?

CHAPTER 3

"The Doctor is in"

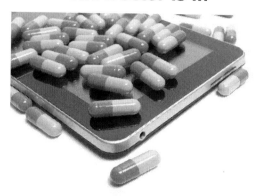

Smartphone addict (n):

Anyone whose smartphone use has become so excessive, disruptive, and deeply ingrained in their life that it creates conflict for him or her and others around them.

Americans and people from all over the world really, really, really love their cell phones. Many spend more time with their phone than they do with their friends or romantic partner, but can you be addicted to a piece of technology? What was your score on the cell phone addiction scale in the previous chapter? Still not convinced that you can actually be addicted to your iPhone or Galaxy S6? Because I know you still might be skeptical I decided to ask a number of health care professionals and experts in the area of addiction their thoughts on the subject. I asked each of them the same four questions:

1. Can someone be addicted to their cell phone? Why or why not?
2. What signs or symptoms would you look for when deciding if someone is addicted to their cell phone?
3. What is one suggestion you could offer to help someone control their cell phone use?
4. Are you addicted to your cell phone? Why or why not?

I think you will find what these professionals have to say about the possibility of cell phone addiction very interesting. So, onto the interviews...

Sharon W. Stern, M.D.
Medical Director At Baylor Health Services

Can someone be addicted to their cell phone? Why or why not? Yes. Many people feel lost and anxious when they do not have their cell phone—especially if they do not know where it is.

What signs or symptoms would you look for when deciding if someone is addicted to their cell phone? Signs of anxiety/withdrawal—increase in blood pressure and heart rate, sweating, increased respiratory rate and difficulty concentrating without their cell phone.

What is one suggestion you could offer to help someone better control their cell phone use? Have certain times of day every day where your cell phone is not with you—mealtimes, family time, game nights and, of course, while in bed.

Are you addicted to your cell phone? Why or why not? I am definitely addicted to my cell phone (although it seems to be connected to my anxiety about being reachable by family in case of emergency). I hate it when I leave my cell phone somewhere and have to do without it; it makes me feel a sense of anxiety and dread which really do not make logical sense in the situation.

Sara Dolan, Ph.D.
Associate Professor, Graduate Program Director, Clinical Psychology, Baylor University.

Can someone be addicted to their cell phone? Why or why not? Yes. The general definition of addiction is using something (or engaging in a behavior) to the extent that it causes harm to work, relationship, health, or mental health. People can engage in cell phone use so much/so often that the person may upset a spouse or partner, may neglect work/relationship responsibilities, etc.

What signs or symptoms would you look for when deciding if someone is addicted to their cell phone? The Diagnostic and Statistical Manual for Mental Disorders, Fifth Edition (DSM 5, which is akin to an encyclopedia for psychiatric disorders) lists criteria for substance use disorder as follows:

1. Taking the substance in larger amounts or for longer than the you meant to
2. Wanting to cut down or stop using the substance but not managing to
3. Spending a lot of time getting, using, or recovering from use of the substance
4. Cravings and urges to use the substance
5. Not managing to do what you should at work, home or school, because of substance use
6. Continuing to use, even when it causes problems in relationships
7. Giving up important social, occupational or recreational activities because of substance use

8. Using substances again and again, even when it puts the you in danger
9. Continuing to use, even when the you know you have a physical or psychological problem that could have been caused or made worse by the substance
10. Needing more of the substance to get the effect you want (tolerance)
11. Development of withdrawal symptoms, which can be relieved by taking more of the substance.

One only needs to endorse three of these symptoms to "earn" a diagnosis of substance use disorder. I can imagine that substituting the words "cell phone" for "substance" could yield symptom endorsement for those who use their cell phones so much/so often that it causes harm. In a similar vein, DSM 5 recognizes the first "behavioral addiction," a non-substance-related addiction, in pathological gambling. Its criteria are as follows:

1. Needs to gamble with increasing amounts of money in order to achieve the desired excitement.
2. Is restless or irritable when attempting to cut down or stop gambling.
3. Has made repeated unsuccessful efforts to control, cut back, or stop gambling.
4. Is often preoccupied with gambling (e.g., having persistent thoughts of reliving past gambling experiences, handicapping or planning the next venture, thinking of ways to get money with which to gamble).
5. Often gambles when feeling distressed (e.g., helpless, guilty, anxious, depressed).
6. After losing money gambling, often returns another day to get even ("chasing" one's losses).

7. Lies to conceal the extent of involvement with gambling.
8. Has jeopardized or lost a significant relationship, job, or educational or career opportunity because of gambling.
9. Relies on others to provide money to relieve desperate financial situations caused by gambling.

One needs to endorse four or more of these symptoms to warrant a diagnosis. Although the criteria for pathological gambling are specific to gambling-related behaviors, like "chasing losses," one can see similarities to the criteria for substance use disorder. For example, #2 in the substance use disorder criteria is very similar to #3 in the pathological gambling criteria. I use the example of pathological gambling to illustrate that there are addictive disorders that are more behavioral than alcohol or drug related.

Additionally, research on addiction demonstrates some neurobiological similarities across those with drug use disorders and pathological gambling. I find it entirely reasonable to suggest that if one can be addicted to a behavior like gambling, one can be addicted to a behavior like cell phone use, if it causes the same kinds of occupational, relational, and mental health consequences as drug addictions.

> **What is one suggestion you could offer to help someone better control their cell phone use?** *Try to figure out what need the cell phone is fulfilling and then attempt to fulfill that need in a healthier way. For example, if it is to reduce anxiety in social situations, practice relaxation and/or mindfulness techniques when one would look at his/her cell phone instead. One way to try to figure this out would be to diary one's use of his or her cell phone, and whenever there is an instance of looking at the cell phone, log what thoughts and feelings were also being experienced. Over some time, patterns in*

thoughts, feelings, and cell phone behaviors will start to emerge, and one can begin to substitute healthier behaviors when those thoughts and feelings emerge.

Are you addicted to your cell phone? Why or why not? *Technically, I do not meet three criteria from the substance use disorder criteria list above, so I do not qualify for a diagnosis. Research that establishes what "normal" amounts of cell phone usage will be interesting, as will research that establishes what "cell phone-specific behaviors" can be considered problematic, a la the pathological gambling criteria.*

Wade C. Rowatt, Ph.D.
Professor, Department Of Psychology & Neuroscience, Baylor University

Can someone be addicted to their cell phone? Why or why not? *Humans have a fundamental need to belong and to stay connected with family and friends. To the degree we're using phones to establish or maintain healthy social connections, I see cell and smartphones as a marvelous invention. To the degree cell phones interfere with everyday responsibilities or lead to significant distress, then they can be a serious problem.*

Yes, someone could be addicted to a cell or smartphone if it leads to one or more of the following:

1. Failure to fulfill important obligations at school, work, or home (e.g., repeated absences, poor work performance, neglect of children or household responsibilities)
2. Use in situations in which it's hazardous (i.e., text messaging while driving an automobile)
3. Continued use despite social or interpersonal problems (e.g., arguments with a parent about frequency of use) (Note: these points above parallel criteria for "substance abuse" in the DSM. I think they transfer well to other con-

texts in which addiction could occur).

What signs or symptoms would you look for when deciding if someone is addicted to their cell phone? See above.

What is one suggestion you could offer to help someone better control their cell phone use? *It's remarkably important for people to set reasonable limits on the places and amount of time to use a cell or smartphone for nonwork related activities. Allowing children and teens to have some say in the limits increases their sense of autonomy and freedom (and the likelihood they'll internalize the limits). If a parent just coldly barks an order, it's likely to backfire and alienate the child or teen from a well-intentioned guideline or protection.*

Are you addicted to your cell phone? Why or why not? *I do enjoy using my smartphone to connect with family and friends. So far I've been able to resist the temptation to use it while driving or during long meetings, but everyone gets depleted and needs a social snack from time to time. If we socially snack (e.g., check social media for a few minutes at work), does that mean we're addicted? If it's causing significant impairment or distress, yes. If not, it's OK as long as we're setting limits*

Also, if I may share a personal story. On July 5, 2011 I was in a serious car accident caused by a young woman who was texting while driving on the interstate. Traffic came to a complete stop and she didn't until she slammed into the back of my car at a high rate of speed. Fortunately the airbags and advanced designs protected us both and we were not physically injured. We were both psychologically traumatized for a while. She'd just experienced a relationship breakup and was seeking solace from her support system. She was wise to activate her support system, but needed to do so at an appropriate and safer time and place.

Donald L. Corley, Ph.D.
Clinical Psychologist, Waco, Tx

Can someone be addicted to their cell phone? Why or why not? *Yes. I haven't actually seen a copy of the DSM 5 but according to the National Institute on Drug Abuse (NIDA) the new DSM 5 collapses the terms abuse and addiction into a single category for substances—substance use disorder. When you look at the criteria, there has to be at least two of the following within the past 12 months to justify the diagnosis:*

- The substance was taken in larger amounts or over a longer period than was intended
- A persistent desire or unsuccessful effort to cut down or control use of substance
- A great deal of time is spent in activities necessary to obtain the substance, use the substance, or recover from its effects
- Craving, or a strong desire or urge to use the substance
- Recurrent use of the substance resulting in a failure to fulfill major role obligations at work, school or home
- Continued use of the substance despite having persistent or recurrent social or interpersonal problems caused or exacerbated by the effects of its use
- Important social, occupational, or recreational activities are given up or reduced because of use of the substance
- Recurrent use of the substance in situations in which it is physically hazardous
- Use of the substance is continued despite knowledge of having a persistent or recurrent physical or

psychological problem that is likely to have been caused or exacerbated by the substance
- Tolerance, as defined either by a need for markedly increased amounts of the substance to achieve intoxication or desired effect; or, a markedly diminished effect with continued use of the same amount of the substance
- Withdrawal, as manifested either by withdrawal syndrome or taking the substance to relieve or or avoid withdrawal

So, as you can see, there are a number of these same dynamics that are present in cell phone use and therefore, in my opinion, can cause some of the same problems seen in substance use, gambling, pornography, etc.

What signs or symptoms would you look for when deciding if someone is addicted to their cell phone? In an article by J. Block in the *American Journal of Psychiatry*, (2008) Internet addiction is becoming more clinically recognized because of four primary variants: 1) excessive use, often associated with a loss of time or a neglect of basic drives; 2) withdrawal, including feelings of anger, tension, and/or depression when the computer is inaccessible; 3) tolerance, including the need for better computer equipment, more software, or more hours of use; 4) negative repercussions, including arguments, lying, poor achievement, social isolation and fatigue. I see the same symptoms with cell phones as computers.

What is one suggestion you could offer to help someone better control their cell phone use?

- Take vacation hours or even days so that the cravings subside for periods of time

- Engage in activities that you cannot do with a phone: swimming and other various forms of exercise, reading books, not eBooks, conversing with friends... anything that is a "competitive behavior." This is an essential element in a behavioral control technique called "habit reversal."

Are you addicted to your cell phone? Why or why not? No. I don't use social media because I value my privacy. I think having lived most of my life without a cell phone, I have always valued it as a convenience not a necessity.

Peter Smetaniuk
Behavioral Research Psychologist
B.A. In Psychology, San Francisco, Ca.

Can someone be addicted to their cell phone? Why or why not? Indeed yes; but, we need to be careful when using the word addiction dealing with virtual technologies. Many people confuse the frequency of smartphone use with addiction. It's not the frequency, but rather what criteria are fulfilled because of its use. Cell phone use becomes problematic, in my opinion, when the individual is self-aware they are using their phones too much and is interfering with their daily activities.

For example, do they feel anxious when they are not on their phones, do they experience psychological salience (thinking about using their phones constantly throughout the day), when they are upset or bored do they use their phones as a mood modifier (or escapism), and finally, if they are already clinically depressed, then cell phone use can truly be a pacifier. Hence, there is a strong relationship between depression and problematic cell phone use (e.g., late night web browsing, online gambling, online gaming, increased social networking, and etc.). In sum, if the user is self-aware and they have a difficult time controlling their use, we can say they have a clinical type of mental disorder called impulse control disorder (ICD).

What signs or symptoms would you look for when deciding if someone is addicted to their cell phone? Of course, the causes of many of the symptoms are not easily identifiable as an effect of cell phone use. But there are red flags waving when a person is at a social gathering and they can't take their eyes off that little screen—when they do, they become quite moody or irritable (a form of anxiety where they think they are missing out on something—especially if they frequent social networks and text constantly).

Note: The list of criteria (or symptoms) are also listed in my manuscript. If an individual scores or fulfills 5 out of 10 criteria relative to adverse experiences, then they are considered problematic users.

What is one suggestion you could offer to help someone better control their cell phone use? I also did an actual experiment with participants shutting down their cells for 3 days. I wanted to measure their psychological and physiological stress levels over the 3 day period. At the end of the study I crunched the numbers for "before and after" results and there were no differences in stress levels. This experiment was difficult to do because the ethical review board did not allow me to have participants with high blood pressure (Helsinki protocols so to speak). I decided to continue with the study but excluded all participants with a history of heart problems, diabetics, or high blood pressure.

All my participants had very healthy blood pressure readings, so of course there blood pressure did not decrease. Initially I predicted that taking a cell phone away or minimizing cell phone use would lower blood pressure (the statistical analysis or psychometric analysis in hypothesis testing)—thus, my hypothesis never went to manuscript. Nevertheless, part of the experiment called for interviewing each participant in the experimental group and how they felt about not using their phones for 3 days (the qualitative analysis). Interestingly, almost all of them claimed it was a "breath of fresh air," "a huge weight off their shoulders," "an anchor" they thought they couldn't control—but now can.

And finally, they enjoyed the fact they can control their cell phone use—a "newfound feeling of empowerment." That said, one way to help someone with bettering their overuse may be to simply shut off one's phone for a while throughout the day: When eating, when socializing with friends and family, when walking in public (we've all seen those dangers on YouTube videos), when going to sleep for the night, and when on vacation). Of course for some, this may be difficult. But it's requiring that the person have some self-control over their behaviors—if and only if—their cell phone use is troublesome to them.

Are you addicted to your cell phone? Why or why not? A big NO! I rarely use my phone. Then again, as I mentioned in my article, age is also a determining factor for problematic use. I'm 60 years of age and don't rely on my cell too much for anything—I carry it for emergency purposes only. I even have control over my emailing—which is mostly done sitting at my desk, at home. Simply put, I do web browsing for academic purposes, but I'm also aware of the time I spend on the computer and break away from it when it becomes fatiguing.

Dr. Mark Griffiths
Professor Of Gambling Studies,
Director Of International Gaming Research Unit,
Psychology Division,
Nottingham Trent University, UK

Can someone be addicted to their cell phone? Why or why not? *That depends on how 'addiction' is defined. I believe that anything can be potentially addictive if constant rewards and reinforcement are present. Some people may confuse habitual use of such technology as an addictive behaviour (when in reality it may not be). For instance, some people may consider themselves cell phone addicts because they never go out of the house without their cell phone, do not turn their cell phone off at night, are always expecting calls from family members or friends, and/or over-utilise cell phones in their work and/or social life.*

There is also the importance of economic and/or life costs. The crucial difference between some forms of cell phone use and pathological cell phone use is that some applications involve a financial cost. If a person is using the application more and is spending more money, there may be negative consequences as a result of not being able to afford the activity (e.g., negative economic, jobrelated, and/or family consequences). High expenditure may also be indicative of cell phone addiction but the phone bills of adolescents are often paid for by parents, therefore the financial problems may not impact on the users themselves.

It is very difficult to determine at what point cell phone use becomes an addiction. The cautiousness of researchers suggests that we are not yet in a position to confirm the existence of a serious and persistent psychopathological addictive disorder related to cell phone addiction on the basis of population survey data alone. This cautiousness is aided and supported by other factors including: (a) the absence of any clinical demand in accordance with the percentages of problematic users identified by these investigations, (b) the fact that the psychometric instruments used could be measuring 'concern' or 'preoccupation' rather than 'addiction, (c) the normalisation of behaviour and/or absence of any concern as users grow older; and (d) the importance of distinguishing between excessive use and addictive use.

What signs or symptoms would you look for when deciding if someone is addicted to their cell phone? *You could argue that a person is no more addicted to their phone than an alcoholic is addicted to the bottle. Individuals tend to have addictions on their mobile phone rather than to their phone. For me to class someone as addicted to their mobile phone they would have to fulfill the following six criteria:*

1. **Salience**—This occurs when the mobile phone use becomes the single most important activity in the person's life and dominates their thinking (preoccupations and cognitive distortions), feelings (cravings) and behaviour (deterioration of socialised behaviour). For instance, even if the person is not actually on their phone they will be constantly thinking about the next time that they will be (i.e., a total preoccupation with their mobile phone).

2. **Mood modification**—This refers to the subjective experiences that people report as a consequence of mobile phone use and can be seen as a coping strategy (i.e., they experience an arousing 'buzz' or a 'high' or paradoxically a tranquilizing feel of 'escape' or 'numbing') when on the phone.

3. **Tolerance**—This is the process whereby increasing amounts of mobile phone use are mobile phone users gradually build up the amount of the time they spend on

their phone every day.

1. **Withdrawal symptoms**—These are the unpleasant feeling states and/or physical effects (e.g., the shakes, moodiness, irritability, etc.) that occur when the person is unable to use their phone because there is no signal, mislaid or broken phone, etc.

2. **Conflict**—This refers to the conflicts between the person and those around them (interpersonal conflict), conflicts with other activities (social life, hobbies and interests) or from within the individual themselves (intra-psychic conflict and/or subjective feelings of loss of control) that are concerned with spending too much on their mobile phone.

3. **Relapse**—This is the tendency for repeated reversions to earlier patterns of excessive mobile phone use to recur and for even the most extreme patterns typical of the height of excessive mobile phone use to be quickly restored after periods of control.

What is one suggestion you could offer to help someone better control their cell phone use? I don't have a single suggestion. If there was a single suggestion to overcome or better control problematic phone use then I could give up my whole research career ☺.

My tips on digital detox can be found here: http://www.addiction.com/expert-blogs/12-tips-for-a-digital-detox/

Are you addicted to your cell phone? Why or why not? No, because I don't have one. I gave up my mobile phone years ago.

Who: Dr. Michael B. Frisch
Professor Of Psychology,
Department Of Psychology And Neuroscience,
Baylor University

Dr. Frisch has been a practicing and supervising clinical and positive psychologist for thirty years with experience in working in addictions and other DSM disorders.

Can someone be addicted to their cell phone? Why or why not? *Yes, you can be addicted to your cell phone or have a problem with compulsive use of your cell phone, the preferred term for psychologists. Pathological gambling is now a DSM disorder in the "addiction" section, so cell phone use, disordered eating, and other behaviors can also be seen as "addictions" or compulsive behaviors.*

What signs or symptoms would you look for when deciding if someone is addicted to their cell phone? *Take the following test to determine if you have cell phone addiction:*

Cat Or Cell Phone Addiction Test™

1. People close to me have complained about my cell phone use.
   ☐Yes   ☐No
2. My time on my cell phone interferes with me getting important work done.
   ☐Yes   ☐No
3. My time on my cell phone interferes with my relationships.
   ☐Yes   ☐No
4. My time on my cell phone gets in the way of me carrying out my obligations.
   ☐Yes   ☐No

5. My time on my cell phone has gotten me in trouble at work, school, or home.
   ☐Yes   ☐No
6. I am worried or upset about the amount of time I spend on my cell phone.
   ☐Yes   ☐No
7. I am worried or upset about what I do while on my cell phone.
   ☐Yes   ☐No

© (April 18, 2015) Michael B. Frisch. Reprinted by permission.

Scoring instructions: *If you answered "yes" to two or more questions, you have a "problem" with your cell phone use which could be an "addiction" should it persist for six months or longer. A physician and/or a mental health therapist who specializes in addiction or compulsive behaviors should be consulted if your problem persists for six months or longer.*

The CAT is based upon current views of addiction, substance use and abuse, and compulsive behavior, including the DSM-5 and related articles and tests like the Michigan Alcohol Screening Test or MAST.

What is one suggestion you could offer to help someone better control their cell phone use? *Keep a cell phone use diary with the date, time, duration, and type of cell phone activity you are engaged in at any given time such as games or Facebook. Look for patterns in your diary and experiment with increasing or decreasing time in activities that seem to create problems for you. Share your diary with trusted friends who do not seem to have a problem with their cell phone use; get their advice on how to get better control.*

Are you addicted to your cell phone? Why or why not? *I do not have a problem with cell phone addiction* because I answered "no" to all eight questions on the CAT or Cell phone Addiction Test™. That is, cell phone use is not interfering with my relationships or with my ability to carry out obligations and pursue hobbies.

April Lane Benson, Ph.D.
Founder of Stopping Overshopping, LLC, NYC, NY

April Benson, Ph.D., is a nationally known psychologist specializing in the study and treatment of compulsive buying disorder. She is the founder of Stopping Overshopping, LLC and author of To Buy or Not to Buy: Why We Overshop and How to Stop. For more information, go to shopaholicnomore.com.

Can someone be addicted to their cell phone? Why or why not? Most definitely someone can be addicted to his or her cell phone. According to these commonly accepted definitions, addiction is

- A strong and harmful need to regularly have something (such as a drug) or do something (such as gamble).

- The compulsive use of a substance despite ongoing negative consequences, which may lead to tolerance or withdrawal symptoms when the substance is stopped.

Some people regularly need to have their cell phone in hand, and on hand, but don't necessarily need to use it all the time. Others need more active and constant engagement with their cell phones. They might be talking, texting, emailing, browsing the internet, ordering pizza, getting directions, listening to music, playing games, or using them in a thousand different ways. In and of itself, none of this is necessarily compulsive or addictive.

It's only when the consequences of the cell phone use are consistently negative and the individual can't stop or may even keep accelerating his or her use of the cell phone that it becomes seriously problematic. The individual's attachment to the cell phone may be so strong that meaningful exchanges between people and real relationships are receding farther and further into the background. In addition to those interpersonal consequences, there can be serious financial consequences. There's no end to the amount of money one can spend purchasing goods and services via the cell phone. Compulsive cell phone use sometimes results in an individual's missing important appointments, events, information or opportunities, all of which have negative aftereffects, and can trigger anxiety, shame or guilt. Some people engage in secret trysts which then prove to be traceable, extremely anxiety provoking, and damaging to relationships and careers. Others incessantly look for information about a medical condition that hasn't even been confirmed and feel depressed as a result.

As far as tolerance or withdrawal symptoms when the substance is stopped, there are certainly people whose functioning suffers when they're not able to use their cell phone because of some external rule (e.g., no cell phone in class or at the movies) or external condition (no cell service in a particular location). They might become withdrawn, angry, restless or anxious, seemingly way out of proportion with the catalyst.

What signs or symptoms would you look for when deciding if someone is addicted to their cell phone? *Troublesome signs or symptoms to look for are someone being on their cell phone constantly and using the cell phone to escape something challenging or painful in his or her life. You might also see mood changes, especially increased irritability and isolation, when someone isn't able to use the cell phone. The need to have the cell phone by the bedside, walking and using a cell phone constantly are other red flags. Think about what it's like when someone is using their cell phone in an elevator or when they're at the check out counter at the grocery, what that does to our social fabric of our society, repeated millions of times over? When attachment to the cell phone trumps attachment to people, animals, hobbies,* there is very good reason to be concerned. It's particularly worrisome if the person has tried to cut back on cell phone use, but hasn't been able to.

What is one suggestion you could offer to help someone better control their cell phone use? As with any addiction, availability is one of the biggest risk factors for not gaining control of any harmful habit or pattern. That said, spending cell phone free time, forcing yourself if you have to, is critical. Making the decision to leave your cell phone at home and giving yourself the opportunity to have experiences where your sustained attention brings joy.

Texting is not a nuanced communication and misunderstandings and misinterpretations are rampant. Looking squarely at the negative effects that some of your texts or emails have had can be a strong motivation to minimize this form of communication and pick up the phone or have face to face contact.

All of this is difficult to do totally on one's own. Ask someone to function as your support buddy and brainstorm the ways that you and your buddy are going to work together to help you control your cell phone use. You two might work on a goal related to how much time you'll have your cell phone around and how much time you'll use it, if you do have it on your person. You two might decide on a cell-free evening or day together and think through together how you're going to spend that time and how you'll manage any yearnings for your cell phone or impulses to go get it.

All of this said, there are ways of turning this technology on its ear. In the last few years, digital health and mental health interventions in the form of apps and text messaging programs have been used effectively for a variety of problems like smoking cessation, diabetes management, reduced alcohol consumption, bulimic behavior, and now, compulsive buying disorder.

Are you addicted to your cell phone? Why or why not? *I'm not addicted to my cell phone because I don't spend at lot of time on it. I use it mostly for talking to people, texting, using my calendar, using the timer, and taking photos and videos. Occasionally I'll listen to a podcast. I don't really like using it to check emails and write emails, so I keep that to a minimum. I do play one game on it, Scrabble. Sometimes I purposely go to places where there's no cell reception so that I can unplug for a while and connect more intimately with other people and with myself, use the time to enjoy new activities and to meditate. However, even if I'm unplugged from my cell phone, I need to take care not to use my computer in a similar way. That said, it's time for me to get off this computer and go meditate!*

A Few Observations On The Experts' Opinions

I have polled the experts and the diagnosis is in: Yes, you can be addicted to your smartphone. Psychologists, psychiatrists, medical doctors, and academics alike who either treat people in the throes of addiction or who do research to better understand addiction all seem to be speaking with one voice. Addiction is no longer limited to substances but includes addiction to such things as our cell phones.

Signs of smartphone addiction, experts say, include anxiety, increased in blood pressure and heart rate and difficulty concentrating when you're separated from your smartphone. Are you moody or irritable when separated from your smartphone? If you are, you might be addicted. Eyes glued to your screen in a variety of social situations? You guessed it; you might be addicted to your cellular lifeline. Dr. Griffith (UK addiction expert) listed the six signs of cell phone addiction discussed in chapter two and he should since he was the one to originally come up with this list of the core components of cell phone addiction.

Addiction expert, Sara Dolan, listed the 11 criteria for substance use disorder as laid out in the Diagnostic Statistical Manual for Mental Disorders (DSM5). The DSM5 is the "bible" for identifying and treating mental disorders. She mentions that if you said "yes" to only three of any of the eleven criteria you could be considered "addicted." Dr. Frisch even offered his own cell phone addiction scale (CAT). Did your score on his scale seem to agree with your score from my scale in chapter two? My guess is that they both were pretty close.

The experts also seem to agree on ways to help someone reduce their reliance on their smartphone. As I suggest later in chapter ten of this book, all experts feel establishing cell phone free times and places can help you regulate your smartphone use. Dr. Corley (clinical psychologist) suggests taking time away from your phone so your cravings will subside. Or, engage in activities that you cannot do with your smartphone: swim or other types of exercise and especially any type of "competitive behavior." Dr. Dolan makes an interesting suggestion by asking you to identify the need your smartphone fulfills and trying to fill this need in a healthier way. If you are spending too much time on social media because you're lonely, you may try to fulfill your need for companionship by physically getting together with a friend for a coffee or a friends night out on a regular basis.

On a positive note, Peter Smetaniuk conducted an experiment where subjects shut down their cell phones for three days. I know, amazing that he was able to entice anyone to participate. Interestingly, the majority of those who lasted the 3-day detox reported that the three days away from their smartphones was like a "breath of fresh air," that a "huge weight" had been lifted from their shoulders, and they now felt "empowered"—they were now in control of their cell phone rather than vice versa. Three days is a big "gulp" but try a "sip" by establishing "smartphone-free" times and you may experience some of the wonderful sensations and sense of empowerment reported by Smetaniuk's subjects.

Physician, Dr. Stern, was the only expert who reported feeling like she was addicted to her cell phone. She felt her attachment to her cell phone was tied to her anxiety and worries over the safety of her family. That she needed to be able to be reached in case of emergencies. These needs to be safe and reachable were the long-forgotten reasons behind the need for cell phones. Dr. Griffith's reports that he doesn't even own a cell phone and Peter Smetaniuk rarely uses his while the others appear to have their smartphone use under control. I enjoyed Dr. Rowatt's personal aside about being hit in his car by a young woman talking on her smartphone. I was touched by his compassion for the young woman but also noted his call to refrain from smartphone use while driving an automobile.

For me, this may be the most exciting chapter in this book. The opportunity to hear from people on the front lines of addiction treatment and research is priceless. I leave this chapter with a renewed sense that technologies such as cell phones can be addictive and present signs that we all can recognize. And, that mitigating the damage caused by such addictions may be as simple (at least in theory) as setting aside time in your day when smartphones and electronics are banned from your presence. Please read chapter ten of this book for more ideas on how to better manage your relationship with your smartphone.

Food for Thought

1. Do you agree with the experts on whether you can be addicted to your cell phone? Why or why not?
2. Do you exhibit any of the symptoms of cell phone addiction discussed by the experts? Which one(s)?
3. Can someone be addicted to their cell phone? Why or why not?
4. After reading chapters 2 and 3 do you see signs of cell phone addiction in any of your family members or friends?

What is one area in which you need to cut back on your cell phone use? Any plans for doing so?

CHAPTER 4

TO Phubb Or Not To Phubb

"My life has become a major distraction from my cell phone"

— *Anonymous*

If it can happen to the Great Beyonce´, then it can happen to you and me. The image is seared into my long-term memory. As seen on the daily mail.com website, Hip-hop Mogul and rap superstar, Jay-Z, is seen checking out the latest breaking news on his cell phone while the Great Beyonce´ cools her heels in the background—a shell of her attention-grabbing stage persona. And, I am reasonably sure that all of us have been both the phubber and the phubbee.

Here's a big word for you: Portmanteau. A Portmanteau is a word that is a combination of two words being smashed together. In the present case, phubbing is a splicing together of the words "phone" and "snubbing."[29] To be phubbed is to be snubbed by someone using their cell phone while in your company. The "phubb" could be an interruption of your conversation with someone when he or she uses their cell phone or is distracted by it (furtive glances when they think you're not looking) instead of paying attention to you. Maybe worse, you've been phubbed if someone used their cell phone instead of communicating with you while in close proximity to you. Oh, the shame!

Do you phubb people?
☐ Yes   ☐ No

Have you been phubbed?
☐ Yes   ☐ No

I gave you a choice with the first question, but I know the answer to the second. We've all been phubbed repeatedly and we don't like it. In the next two chapters we will talk about whether your cell phone use causes conflict in your life and whether your love life might be a bit better off with a little less phubbing.

But for now the spotlight is going to remain on you and your phubbing tendencies. My good friend and colleague, Dr. Meredith David, and I have developed a nine-item phubbing scale and you now have the opportunity to do a little self-assessment by answering the phubbing questions that appear below.[30] You can easily score yourself and see where you fall on the phubbing continuum.

Please be honest when responding to the nine phubbing statements. You will not be asked to turn in your work (remember I am a college professor) and this will only be helpful if you take an "eyes wide-open" approach to your self-evaluation. Simply check "yes" or "no" to each of the phubbing statements.

Are You a Phubber?

1. When I am having a meal with others (at home or in a restaurant) I will pull out and check my cell phone.
   ☐ Yes   ☐ No
2. I always have my cell phone in sight when I am spending time with others.
   ☐ Yes   ☐ No
3. I often keep my cell phone in my hand when I am with others.
   ☐ Yes   ☐ No
4. If my cell phone rings or beeps I will pull it out and check even if I am talking with someone.
   ☐ Yes   ☐ No
5. I have been caught glancing at my cell phone when talking to someone.
   ☐ Yes   ☐ No
6. When I am hanging with friends I don't hesitate to check my cell phone if I am bored or get a text, or other notification.
   ☐ Yes   ☐ No
7. I will use my cell phone when I am talking with friends.
   ☐ Yes   ☐ No
8. I use my cell phone when I am on a date or with my romantic partner.
   ☐ Yes   ☐ No
9. If there is a lull in a conversation, I will diddle with my cell phone.
   ☐ Yes   ☐ No

Bonus Question:

I have used my cell phone in bed while my partner was present.

☐ Yes   ☐ No

This last question is not an official part of the phubbing scale, but might, in my humble estimation, be the worst phubb of them all. So, Are You a Phubber?

This is where the rubber meets the road. Have you been dishing out more than your fair share of phubbs or have you learned to navigate the stormy waters of socially acceptable cell phone use?

To calculate your score, simply add up the number of "yes" responses to each of the nine statements and check how you did below.

Results Key:

6+ "Yes" answers: I will personally make a reservation for you at the Betty Ford Clinic for habitual cell phone users.

3-5 "Yes" answers: You are not there yet but are on the edge of the slippery slope of phubbing.

1-2 "Yes" answers: You are a master of cell-control or you don't have any friends (just kidding).

Food for Thought

1. Do you think you are a problem phubber? Why or why not?
2. Was your phubbing score accurate? Why or why not?
3. Has phubbing ever got you into trouble?
4. How do you feel when you're phubbed?
5. Is phubbing a big problem in general?

As we will discuss in the next two chapters, how we use cell phones can either avoid or create conflict, and get ready for this, even lead to less satisfying romantic relationships. To find out how, you need to read chapter six.

Chapter 5

Cell Phone Purgatory

"Apparently we love our own cell phones but we hate everyone else's"

— Joe Bob Briggs
(American film critic and writer)

What do you think; does your cell phone use impact your relationship with your romantic partner? Mike Green of Mankato, Minnesota, would regrettably answer "yes" to this question. It started out innocently enough as reported by Jennifer Ludden of NPR. In 2005, his then-wife Lyn (know where this story is going) asked to add texting to their cell phone plan—oh, the good old days.

It must have been a rhetorical question because she went ahead and signed up for it without Mike's approval and was soon texting like a pimply-faced teenager in love—maybe too much. Perusing their cell phone bill, Mike noticed one number more than others kept popping up. You guessed it. Mike's ex was having an affair with a co-worker who she eventually left Mike for. Mike commented that he was shocked how quickly his then-wife's texting partner turned into her snuggle bunny.

One expert was not surprised. Bob Rosenwein of Lehigh University claims that online relationships often turn into something more in about a week—talk about hot pants. Face-to-face communications take two to three times longer to come to a full boil. Surprisingly, since his divorce, Mike is now texting and a denizen of various social media sites. Yet, his trust has been broken and he is wary of future romantic relationships. Mike is back in the dating game but still gets suspicious every time his current partner sends a text. Once, bitten, twice shy.[31]

Your spouse may not have cheated on you via his or her cell phone, but cell phones are still a major distraction in relationships. I am not sure how many of you are having intimate encounters with your romantic partner, but I do know that 65 percent of adult Americans have slept with their cell phone. To make matters worse, we spend a lot more time with our cell phones than we do with our partners. A research study I conducted with my dearly departed friend and co-author, Chris Manolis, found that college students spend about eight hours every day on their phones.

Non-college age adults aren't far behind. And, here's the punch line, how much time do US adults spend with their partners? One study says a measly 97 minutes per day. You don't have to be a rocket scientist to see where the problem might lie. The constant distractions caused by our cell phones can undermine our very happiness. A stable and healthy romantic relationship is the cornerstone of happy individuals and well-adjusted families. As the old saying goes, "when momma's not happy, nobody is happy." So, how are we doing in the marital/relationship satisfaction department? Not so good. The US divorce rate hovers somewhere around 45 percent. And, not to add fuel to the fire, but satisfaction rates within intact marriages and relationships have been dropping like a lead balloon.

Not that cell phones and other technologies are the only culprits in our dismal relationship record, but research suggests that in many instances they are not helping. Distractions of any sort, regardless of their cause, can undermine the formation of healthy relationships. Technoference is the term given to the inevitable intrusions and interruptions caused by technology when we are trying to interact or spend time with our romantic partner. With the ever-increasing presence and use of cell phones, the boundaries that separate other interests and partner relationships have become increasingly "blurred." There is no book on technology etiquette (not until chapter eight of this book) and couples are left to navigate these stormy and somewhat murky waters on their own.

A groundbreaking study published in 2014 by the duo of Brandon McDaniel and Sarah Coyne found that technoference (interruptions by all types in technology, not just cell phones) not only decreased how satisfied women were with their relationships but also increased their likelihood of being depressed and decreased their over-all satisfaction with life. When you allow technology to interrupt your conversations and time spent with your romantic partner you send a clear message what's most important to you.[32]

McDaniel and Coyne explain that technology interferes with our ability to connect with our partners in two ways. First, although this sounds like a line from the movie "Her" with Joaquin Phoenix where he falls in love with his Siri-sounding operating system, people can develop "intimate" relationships with their electronic devices at the expense of relationships with real flesh and blood people. A second way technology interferes with the development of healthy human relationships, is that we try to "multi-task" and do both at the same time. Sound familiar? The bad news is that we are lousy multitaskers. We have limited attention spans and something is going to suffer. In a popular book by Sherry Turkle (2012) this has been referred to as "Alone Together." Turkle argues that media such as cell phones is separating people from one another. In essence, partners may be in physical proximity to each other, but not fully present for each other.[33]

For a relationship to be mutually satisfying, each partner must be present for each other. Presence is best understood as a process whereby each member in a relationship stays open and focused on their partner without, and here's the difficult part, external or internal distractions. As humans we are social animals and want to connect with others, especially romantic partners. When we are present, our partner feels connected and safe.

The two most basic human needs are the need for attachment and control. Both of these basic needs are interrupted by phubbing or other technoferences. Being present is central to happy and healthy relationships, but how can we be present when we are constantly distracted by our cell phones? Let me share one last story with you before we talk about a study that I did with Meredith David on phubbing, cell phone conflict, and relationship satisfaction in the next chapter.

We can all easily understand how the constant beeps, bells, and whistles of cell phones can distract us when we are with our loved ones. But, did you know, that even the mere presence of cell phones (when they are not even on) can undermine how close and connected we feel with others?

The research team of Andrew Przybylski and Netta Weinstein of the University of Essex in the UK conducted two experiments in which they manipulated the presence (or absence) of cell phones while a pair of subjects had either casual or meaningful conversations. In the cell phone present condition, a "plain" cell phone was placed on top of a book or a nearby desk outside of the direct line of site of the subjects. In the initial experiment, subjects were asked to spend ten minutes talking about an interesting event that happened in the past month. After their ten minutes were up, the subjects were asked to complete measures of relationship quality and emotional sensitivity.

Another group of subjects had a similar conversation but no cell phone was present (control group). Subjects where the cell phone was present during their conversation reported lower levels of relationship satisfaction and closeness with their discussion partners than did subjects when the cell phone was not present.[34] A second experiment manipulated the content of the discussion. Either the conversation was casual where participants were asked to talk about their thoughts and feelings about plastic Christmas trees or it was more meaningful where the subjects were instructed to talk about the most meaningful events that occurred over the past year.

Again, either the cell phone was present or absent for half the participants. So, you either had a casual conversation and the cell phone was either present or not, or you had a meaningful conversation and the cell phone was either present or not. After their discussions, all subjects were asked to complete measures of relationship quality, whether they trusted their discussion partner and whether they felt their partner was empathetic to their thoughts and feelings.

The findings of this experiment were telling. Once again, the presence of the cell phone undermined relationship quality. When the cell phone was present, participants reported enjoying their relationships less. Also, the presence of a cell phone had a more negative impact when the conversations were meaningful. Subjects reported lower relationship quality and partner trust when the conversation was more meaningful. Perceived empathy was less when a cell phone was present regardless if the conversation was casual or meaningful. So, what does this mean for me and you? It means that cell phones can interfere with perceived relationship quality among couples. And, this is particularly true when people are discussing topics that are personally relevant. Word to the wise, put the cell phone down, better yet, place it out of sight when having important conversations with your romantic partner.

As an added bonus, and at no extra expense to you, I have included a 10 question cell phone conflict scale for you to complete.[35] The scale measures how much conflict (havoc) your cell phone wreaks in your relationship with your romantic partner. Simply circle how often you have experienced the feelings or performed the behaviors described below.

Cell Phone Conflict Scale

This set of questions asks about your partner's cell phone use. Simply circle how often you have experienced the feelings or performed the behaviors described below.

		Never	Rarely	Sometimes	Often	All of the time
1	I have explicitly told my partner about how his/her cell phone use irritates me.	1	2	3	4	5
2	I have talked with my partner about how his/her cell phone use bothers me.	1	2	3	4	5
3	My partner and I argue over his/her cell phone use.	1	2	3	4	5
4	My partner and I cannot agree on when we should use or not use our cell phones	1	2	3	4	5
5	My partner uses his/her cell phone so much when we are together that I often have to ask him/her to put it away.	1	2	3	4	5
6	My partner's use of his/her cell phone when we are together really irritates me.	1	2	3	4	5
7	Although my partner's cell phone use irritates me, I usually ignore it.	1	2	3	4	5
8	I have given up trying to get my partner to not interrupt me by using his/her cell phone when I am talking.	1	2	3	4	5
9	I have checked my partner's cell phone messages without him/her knowing it.	1	2	3	4	5
10	I am sometimes suspicious of my partner's cell phone use.	1	2	3	4	5

Is technoference affecting your relationship? To calculate your score, simply add up your responses to each of the ten statements and check how you did below.

If You Scored... 40-50

A technology intervention is needed immediately. If you see me drive up to your house, it's too late.

30-39

Problems are a brewing but there's still time for redemption. Look for ways to step back from your cell phone. I will talk about something I call Smartphone Smack Down later in this book.

20-29

Not bad. It appears that you have reached some type of understanding with your partner in regards to cell phone use when the two of you are together.

10-19

As a couple, you clearly have a handle on your mutual cell phone use. This is important because it is conflict, not time on one's cell phone that is responsible for its negative impact on relationships.

Food for Thought

1. Has anyone ever broken up with you via text?
2. Do you spend more time on your cell phone than with your romantic partner?
3. Has technoference caused problems in your current relationship?
4. What was your score on the cell phone conflict scale? Does it accurately reflect the tension (or lack thereof) caused by your partner's cell phone use.
5. Does the presence of your cell phone distract you when you are around others?

CHAPTER 6

Partner Phubbing and Relationship Satisfaction

Used with permission by King Dist.

"There's nothing I love more than waking up next to you and a device to check my e-mail"

— *Anonymous*

In Chapter four you bared your soul as to your own phubbing, now you get to see if the problem might partly lie on the other side of the bed from you. Partner phubbing (for here on out referred to as Pphubbing) can be best understood as the extent to which an individual uses or is distracted by his or her cell phone while in the company of his or her relationship partner. Given that nearly every couple uses their cell phones to text each other or communicate via social media, Pphubbing is nearly an inevitable occurrence.

A large scale survey by the PEW Research Center (2,252 respondents) found that 25 percent of cell phone owners in a romantic relationship felt their significant other phubbed them while they were together. This figure jumped to 42 percent for adults ranging in age from 18-29 years old. Despite the fact that this was a large random sample of US adults, I feel the results vastly underestimate the amount of Pphubbing that takes place. In fact, a survey of 143 females involved in romantic relationships conducted by Brandon McDaniel and Sarah Coyne mentioned earlier found that a much higher incidence of Pphubbing.

A full seventy percent of the females reported that cell phones "sometimes," "often," "very often," or "all the time," interfered in their interactions with their partners. Incredibly, a large scale survey of US adults that I conducted with Meredith David of Baylor University found that 59% of the respondents reported that their partners used their cell phones in bed—talk about the thrill is gone.[36]

Studying the impact of phubbing on romantic relationships is critical since happy and healthy relationships lead to happy people and stable families. You are satisfied with your relationship to the degree to which you feel your spouse meets your needs and desires. How we interact with our partners is one, if not the most important, predictor of relationship satisfaction.

There are two, maybe more; theories that can help explain how Pphubbing impacts relationship satisfaction. The first is referred to as the "displacement hypothesis." Very simply, this theory argues that time spent on media, such as cell phones, may displace (or reduce) meaningful interactions with one's spouse. For example, someone who is always fiddling or distracted by their cell phone is not fully present during conversations or shared time together. Research has found that it is not always the preoccupation with the technology itself that causes problems but because it takes away time with one's partner.

I have labeled a second and possibly over-lapping theory, the "conflict hypothesis." A preoccupation with one's cell phone is a source of quarrelling and marital conflict which undermines satisfaction with one's romantic partner.

A study of the impact of technology interference (not just cell phones, but TV, iPads, computers, etc.) found that such interference caused conflict over technology use within romantic partners. This conflict, not surprisingly, negatively impacted relationship satisfaction among their female respondents. The authors concluded that it is not the time spent with technologies that interfered with happy relationships but the conflict created by such technology use. Pphubbing sends a clear message to your partner that they are not as important as all the goodies available through your cell phone. Posting a "hilarious" Instagram picture or pithy comment on Facebook, responding to an "urgent" text, or ignoring your partner completely while you busy yourself on your cell phone is a sure-fire recipe for a contentious relationship.[37]

In a similar vein, Dr. Meredith David and I conducted a study to investigate the impact of Pphubbing on relationship satisfaction among romantic partners—married, shacking up, going out, etc. But first we needed a measure of partner phubbing. Meredith and I wrote a number of statements that reflected being phone snubbed by your partner.[38] You will get a chance to see and complete the entire set of statements at the end of this chapter. Maybe, just maybe, the conflict over cell phone use in your relationship is not all your fault. We also asked the experts, my students, to provide examples of how they have phubbed or been phubbed by friends, romantic partners, and complete strangers.

We conducted a survey of over 300 adults and asked them to tell us how often their romantic partner committed each of the 20 potential phubbs. With a little statistical hocus-pocus we narrowed the scale down to the nine statements you will find at the end of this chapter.

The purpose of part two of our study was to conduct another survey with a different group of adults where we asked them to respond to the partner phubbing items but also scales that measured cell phone conflict (see chapter five), relationship satisfaction, life satisfaction, and depression. Depression? Can our partner's cell phone use really make us depressed? Read on and find out.

The results of our survey told us that when we are phubbed by our partners it creates cell phone-related conflict that reduces our satisfaction with our current relationship. And we know the problems that can arise when we're not happy with our significant other. What really floored me, however, was our finding that being phubbed by our partner decreased our over-all life satisfaction and made us feel more depressed.

So, what should we take away from all of this? It is clear that, even if we act like our partner's distracted behavior doesn't bother us, it does. We feel a little less important and insecure in our relationship. We sense a detachment that loosens the ties that bind. I believe it was Harvey Fierstein (raspy voiced American actor and activist) that said, "I just wanted to be loved, is that so wrong?" No it's not.

Now it's time to see if your partner is a phubber. Be honest but fair. If you later discuss the results with your partner you need to be able to defend your position.

Partner Phubbing Scale and Instructions

These questions ask about how often your relationship partner (i.e., boyfriend, girlfriend, spouse, partner) exhibits certain behaviors (if you are not currently in a relationship, please think of your most recent relationship as you respond to the questions in this study).

		Never	Rarely	Sometimes	Often	All of the time
1	During a typical mealtime that my partner and I spend together, my partner pulls out and checks his/her cell phone.	1	2	3	4	5
2	When my partner's cell phone rings or beeps, he/she pulls it out even if we are in the middle of a conversation.	1	2	3	4	5
3	During leisure time that my partner and I are able to spend together my partner uses his/her cell phone.	1	2	3	4	5
4	My partner glances at his/her cell phone when talking to me.	1	2	3	4	5
5	My partner places his or her cell phone where they can see it when we are together.	1	2	3	4	5
6	My partner keeps his or her cell phone in their hand when he or she is with me.	1	2	3	4	5
7	My partner uses his or her cell phone in bed.	1	2	3	4	5
8	My partner uses his or her cell phone when we are out together.	1	2	3	4	5
9	If there is a lull in our conversation, my partner will check his or her cell phone.	1	2	3	4	5

Please use the scale provided to indicate how frequently your relationship partner engages in each of the following behaviors as it relates to his or her cell phone use.

Have you been phubbed?

Finally, we get to see if your significant other might be partially to blame for any cell phone-related tension in your relationship. To calculate your score, simply add up the number of points for each question and see how your partner stacks up below.

If Your Partner Scored... 36-45
You deserve a lot more R-E-S-P-E-C-T and it all begins with a sitdown with your partner to discuss his or her phubbing behavior. Don't expect to be greeted with open arms; it will be similar to dealing with a cornered wild animal.

27-35
Your partner is on the ledge looking down upon full-blown phubbing behavior. It is your job to talk him or her down from the ledge before jumping.

18-26
In this day and age your partner appears to be holding up his or her end of the bargain. Be on the lookout, however, as the weather can change at any moment. He or she buys an iPhone and you're off to the races.

9-17
I would be pleasantly surprised if anyone scores in this range. It might even be unrealistic to expect someone to do so. At least all the arguments you've been having aren't about your partner's cell phone use.

An Interview with Dawn Wible—Co-Founder of Talk More Tech Less

In my research on cell phones and technology I have had the distinct pleasure of meeting all types of people interested (and often passionate) in how humans interact with technology and how this human/machine interaction affects our everyday lives. One particularly passionate person is Dawn Wible—co-founder (with her husband Matt) of the Talk More Tech Less ministry. As Dawn states on their website, "The 30 day experience is not anti-technology, it's actually designed to help us use technology in a constructive and healthy way." This quote sums up well the approach of this book. Technology is here to stay and has many wonderful and useful things to offer, it can, however, become "too much of a good thing." Please take a few minutes to read the quick Q&A I had with Dawn as she explains what Talk More Tech Less is all about.

> **Jim:** *Please describe your organization.*

> **Dawn:** *Talk More Tech Less exists to bring awareness and action to the issue of tech dependency. We have created a 30 day experience, designed to strengthen relationships while getting our overuse of technology under control. It is a guide to empower individuals, families and groups to find balance, leading to greater connection.*

Jim: *Why did you start this organization?*

Dawn: *Talk More Tech Less was birthed from mentoring and spending time with teenagers. My husband, Matt, runs an organization that mentors young men in outdoor skills and in life. We saw the benefits of getting young men away from all the distraction and overuse of technology, video games, smartphones and computers and getting them outside! At our summer camps we had the young men take breaks from their phones and construct boxes to take home and use with their families.*

Year after year we saw the dependency issues this brought up in the young men, as well as the freedom it eventually allowed them to have. So, we began researching tech dependency and addiction stats and saw the great need in this culture for balance and freedom! There is a crucial conversation happening about tech dependency in our culture; what it's doing to our brains, mind, health, relationships and society as a whole. Despite the conversation happening we are not seeing much action, so we want to be a part of the solution.

Jim: *How does your organization work?*

Dawn: *We have a 30 Day Experience available to help create that balance. Currently The Experience includes:*

- *The Detox Box to place your phone during strategic times each day*
- *Daily Notecards to help guide your journey to healthier relationships & responsible technology usage*
- *Journal for reflection & documentation*
- *Decal to represent and spread this important message Just as technology quickly progresses we plan to grow and move with it to stay effective in order to guide culture towards freedom.*

Jim: *In your experience, what is the biggest obstacle people have when attempting to cut back on their time spent on their cell phone?*

Dawn: *Needing to be available 24/7. Not only is it a habit to be so attached to our devices, but it is so ingrained in our lives that to be away from it has now become foreign. We must realize we can step away, put it down and engage in the life directly in front of us.*

Jim: *Please share a success story (or two) you have had with your organization.*

Dawn: *My first success story is my own. After realizing my family needed this for our own lives and writing the curriculum, we went through the 30 days ourselves. I cannot put into words all the freedom and connection we found, but in the end we never went back to having phones during meals, among other things. It has been a game changer for my home to have a box to put the phone away during meals and other connection times. I am also more aware about being attentive in the moment. When I post something on social media, it's usually after the fact, later after I've lived the moment first.*

Another success story is from a manager of a major outdoor store. He told me the minute I talked to him about Talk More Tech Less his eyes were opened. He looked at his own life, family and habits and realized his need for this program. He has been our biggest supporter in spreading the word. He feels such a connection with getting people outdoors and away from all their technology. He has major influence and is helping change culture.

Jim: *What is different about your digital detox method?*

Dawn: *There are Digital Getaways you can go on to get away from technology, there are "fasts" you can do to unplug, but we all know we need and use technology* *in our everyday lives. Talk More Tech Less is not saying "Don't Tech" and throw your phone out the window. We are saying "tech LESS" and engage more. Our mission is to learn how to use our devices in everyday life while keeping our relationships a priority. Our 30 days trains you how to unplug in real life and how to create an everyday balance with you and those in your life. You can find us at talkmoretechless.com to learn more.*

If you like what you've read, don't hesitate to contact Dawn and see how you can use this great program to enhance your relationships or even foster a more productive workplace. The possibilities for such a program are nearly endless. The video on their website about family and technology brought tears to my eyes and reminded me why I wrote this book. It is never too late to re-order our priorities.

Food for Thought

1. Is your partner a phubber? Why or why not?
2. Do you give more than you receive (does your partner phubb you more than you phubb him or her?
3. Does getting phubbed by your partner bother you? How?
4. Do you and your partner have any rules concerning cell phone use? What are they?
5. Would your relationship benefit from a few rules concerning cell phone use? How?

CHAPTER 7

Miss Manners on Cell Phone Use

Etiquette (n):
The customary code of polite behavior in society or among members of a particular group or profession.

Faux Pas (n):
An embarrassing or tactless act or remark in a social situation.

Could the rude use of our cell phones be considered a barbaric act—a list of synonyms that followed Faux Pas included blunder, gaffe and barbarism? I might be reluctant to go so far as to say that the countless number of faux pas committed by cell phone users on a daily basis are barbaric (with the exception of using your cell phone while driving) but rude, inconsiderate, and thoughtless quickly come to mind.

It felt like it was just yesterday, I had purchased my hot buttered popcorn and Diet Coke and settled into my seat at the local movie theater. Well, you know where this is going. The incessant fiddling with their cell phones by the four young women sitting in front of me grew increasingly worrisome as it continued through the commercials and movie trailers. I was not consoled by the fact that 80 percent of movie-goers surveyed felt it's okay to talk or text during the previews.

Finally, the movie was about to start and I would get to enjoy my $10 investment in peace. This was not to be the case and against the vehement protestations of my wife and daughters I asked the malfeasant to stop her phone play during the movie. This time I lucked out, she grumbled something, walked out of the theater not to return. Score one for the little guy. Most of the time, just like you, I am forced to suffer the indignity of someone else's inconsiderate behavior for the remainder of the movie.

The public use of cell phones has stirred vigorous debates as cell phones take their place atop the digital heap. Using your cell phone at a funeral? In Church? Or, in the bathroom (one survey finds that 50% of people do)? Public cell phone use has become so commonplace that nothing is considered out-of-bounds anymore. How does it make you feel when someone is loudly yacking on their cell phone in a public place (restaurant, movie, in-line, on the bus, subway or train, you choose) failing even to acknowledge your existence? My guess is not very good. Famous sociologist Erving Goffman likens cell phone users to mental patients who treat others as if they didn't exist as objects not worthy of a glance or even acknowledgement of their existence.

In a thoughtful and well written article in a recent issue of the Wall Street Journal, Christine Rosen, senior editor of the New Atlantis, asked if we have morphed into a citizenry of apathetic bystanders. One story she shared to make her point was the story of 20-year old Justin Valdez who was shot dead on a crowded commuter train in San Francisco. The security camera on the train captured it all. Before a round was shot, the gunman wildly brandished his .45 caliber handgun in the air and even pointed it at commuters sitting accross the aisle. What role did cell phones play in this? While the crazy man was making all those wild gestures with a loaded gun, nobody noticed because they were so distracted by their cell phones and laptops that they didn't even notice all the commotion going on. We have become a nation of apathetic bystanders. Glued to our screens we have lost touch with our surroundings and others around us.

What might be worse, as Rosen noted, the easy availability of recording events and sharing them with others has shifted our focus from helping others to documenting the event so we can get at least 100 likes on Facebook or maybe 500,000 views on YouTube if it's a double murder. We have lost our obligation to others, and, as Rosen wisely points out, if we stop helping and keep recording, we risk, "becoming a society not just of apathetic bystanders but of cruel voyeurs."[39] Have you ever recorded an event with your cell phone when you could have helped the situation taking place?

Thank goodness most of us will never be in a life-and-death situation like the one described above, but we can all suffer from the cuts of thousands of small wounds if we don't start to cultivate reasonable habits when it comes to use of our cell phones both in public and private.

Now, I would like to ask you about your feelings as it relates to cell phone etiquette.

Do you think it is appropriate to use your cell phone in the following places and situations?

(Simply check "Yes" or "No"—no waffling.)

		Yes	No
1	In the bathroom?		
2	At funerals?		
3	In church?		
4	On a date?		
5	In bed?		
6	During a wedding?		
7	During a meeting at work?		
8	While driving?		
9	During family meals?		
10	At work or school?		
11	Movies?		
12	While talking with your boss?		
13	While crossing the street?		
14	During face-to-face conversations		
15	While waiting in line?		
16	In the library?		
17	At the cash register?		
18	Keeping the phone in your hand while talking to others?		
19	Placing your phone in front of you during meal times?		
20	In a car with others?		
21	Interrupting conversations to take calls or answer texts?		
22	While driving with others in the car?		
23	While making a purchase at a store?		
24	End a relationship with a text (ouch!)?		
25	When talking to a stranger?		

Now, check whether you have used your cell phone in any of the places or situations listed below.

(Check "Yes" if you have used your cell phone in those places or situations or "No" if you have not.)

		Yes	No
1	In the bathroom?		
2	At funerals?		
3	In church?		
4	On a date?		
5	In bed?		
6	During a wedding?		
7	During a meeting at work?		
8	While driving?		
9	During family meals?		
10	At work or school?		
11	Movies?		
12	While talking with your boss?		
13	While crossing the street?		
14	During face-to-face conversations		
15	While waiting in line?		
16	In the library?		
17	At the cash register?		
18	Keeping the phone in your hand?		
19	Placing your phone in front of you during meal times?		
20	In a car with others?		
21	Interrupting conversations to take calls or answer texts?		
22	While driving with others in the car?		
23	While making a purchase at a store?		
24	End a relationship with a text (ouch!)?		
25	When talking to a stranger?		

I think you can get the most out of this little exercise if you compare the number of situations and places you checked were inappropriate ("no" answers to the first set of behaviors) to use your cell phone with the number of times you said you performed those very behaviors ("yes" to the second set of behaviors) that you earlier said were inappropriate. Let's call this your smartphone etiquette number of disconnects (SEND). How many places did you say it was inappropriate to use a cell phone but later reported you have done so in those situations? If there is a big discrepancy between your attitudes and behavior there is work to be done.

You also have work to do especially if you said "yes" that in most every situation or place it is okay to use your cell phone and later you reported that you have also done so as well. Not everyone agrees with you.

An interesting survey by the Center for the Digital Future found that many Americans feel that using a cell phone during a meal, in a meeting, or in the halls of academia is not acceptable. As you might have guessed, however, these attitudes vary greatly by age group. Not surprisingly, oldsters are less tolerant of cell phones while the youngsters love their cell phones. If you own an iPhone, everything is fair play.

Even the presence of a cell phone during meal time was judged unacceptable by a whopping 62 percent of all respondents. Texting (76%), surfing the web (80%), e-mailing (79%), and talking on the phones (84%) during meals were held in even lower disregard.

Fifty-two percent of respondents told us that having your cell phone on the table during meetings is "not at all appropriate." And texting (79%), surfing the web (81%), e-mailing (76%), and talking on the phone (90%) were also poison to proper social etiquette.

Now, onto a subject close to my heart—the classroom. Fifty-six percent of those polled said it was inappropriate to have your phone on your desk (almost half of students think it's okay). Texting (58%), surfing the web (63%), and e-mailing were over the half-way mark but way too high for my liking.

Eight percent thought it was okay to make calls during class. How is it that I seem to get all of these students in my class?[40]

A different survey conducted by eBay Daily Deals broadened the scope of its survey and unlocked some very interesting results regarding cell phone etiquette. Twenty-seven percent said they would take a call during a face-to-face conversation and 37 percent said not taking a call is worse than phubbing a friend. And here you go, 80% said it's okay to talk on your phone during the previews at a movie theatre. Nearly 90 percent said pedestrians should not text while crossing the street.

I can tell you this that does not hold on college campuses. I am constantly amazed that more students aren't hit when they have their noses in their phones while crossing the roads on campus. My favorite was the young lady, I call her a triple threat, who was driving a scooter, without a helmet, while talking on her phone. But, back to the survey. One-third of respondents admitted to phubbing, 25 percent said it was okay to text during a meeting (don't let your boss see you), 71 percent disapproved of cell phones in the classroom, but 49 percent felt it was okay to text during a movie.

Thank God (pardon the pun), 78 percent felt there was no place for cell phones in church. Only six percent felt it was okay to text and drive yet I have a hard time believing this when I look at my fellow drivers. Seventy-three percent disapproved of texting while on a date at a restaurant. And, texting while talking with someone face-to-face was pooh-poohed by 74 percent of respondents.[41]

The above disparities in opinions as to when it is appropriate to use our cell phones suggests that a universally agreed upon guide for cell phone etiquette is not likely. I did, however, want to share with you what I feel are some solid suggestions for practicing good cell phone etiquette.

The Miss Manners of Cell Phones

Jacqueline Whitmore founded the Protocol School in Palm Beach, Florida in 1997. At first her main draws were business networking and dining etiquette. It was not long, however, before companies were clamoring for a course on the newfangled device that was the source of so many social faux pas—the cell phone. In 2001, it was quaint to hear that "nearly one-third" of all Americans owned cell phones. How did they ever handle the incessant cacophony? Well, let's fast-forward to 2015 and we find Jacqueline still dispensing advice on cell phone protocol. And, she has added the moniker of the "Miss Manners of Cell Phones" to her many titles.[42]

Since chapters 4–6 address the issue of cell phone use (phubbing) and our significant others, I thought you might enjoy the Miss Manners of Cell Phones' five tips on proper cell phone etiquette while on dates.[43]

Cell Phone Etiquette and Dating Tips

1. Be present for your date. By all means make who you are with your top priority. Put away your cell phone and be in the moment.
2. Alert your date that you are expecting an important call and then excuse yourself when the call or text comes in. Keep the call as brief as possible and apologize for your

absence. All other non-emergency calls are verboten.
3. Never place your cell phone on the table. And, as I tell my students, keep your cell phone off and out of sight.
4. On a date you should only use your cell phone for three reasons: to snap a selfie with him or her, show your date an important photo, or to look up a bit of trivia that has you two love birds stumped.
5. Always ask permission to use your cell phone. It is a courtesy that people enjoy and makes them feel respected. If you do take a picture of you and your date, Miss Manners of Cell Phones recommends you ask their permission before posting it to social media.

In sum, very good advice that will keep your date running smoothly until you discover the piece of lettuce between your front teeth.

Now, for the other 166 hours of the week you are not on a date, I have gleaned from my own musings and several websites (Wikihow.com and the dailymail.com) a top-ten list of socially acceptable cell phone use. Before I share the list, however, something needs to be said about attitude. You will only practice good cell phone etiquette if you really want to. Your heart needs to be in the right place. A true concern about the well-being of others is an essential driver of good cell phone etiquette. Without further ado, here are ten golden chestnuts that will keep your cell phone use in its happy place.

Top Ten List of Proper Cell Phone Etiquette[44]

(Channeling Your Inner Miss Manners)

1. If someone says your cell phone use is bugging them you

need to take their suggestion in good faith. Good cell phone etiquette will be a work in progress. Listen to others around you. If you're not on your cell phone it should be easier to do so.

2. Keep a 10-foot barrier between you and others when you're talking on your cell phone. Trust me no one really wants to get into your business.
3. Avoid talking in enclosed spaces even with the 10-foot barrier. The rest of us feel like we are trapped in a burning house and can't get out.
4. Keep your voice down. I know I violate this principle but am working on it.
5. Avoid using your speaker to conduct your conversations. Others don't want to hear you or your friend on the other end of the line (old time saying when there was such a thing as landlines).
6. Turn down the volume (or place phone on vibrate) and no rump-shaker ring tones.
7. Phones are a no-no at meals.
8. Keep a mental list of when you should not use your cell phone. I suggest no selfies with the recently departed, on the toilet, or during a sermon. There's lots of other "off-limits" places for cell phones.
9. Don't hold face-to-face conversations with others while on your phone.
10. For God's sake, and this should be first on this list, no cell phones while driving and that includes hands-free devices. See Chapter eight for more on this subject.

There are other suggestions for good cell phone etiquette that I would have liked to offer, but the thought of a top-ten list was too compelling. I would have added only using your cell phone when absolutely necessary, watch your language when in a public place, and always ask for permission and forgiveness when you need to use your phone when involved in a face-toface conversation.

Food for Thought

1. Do you feel most people practice good cell phone etiquette? Why or why not?
2. Do you practice good cell phone etiquette?
3. Do you use your phone at the movies? In the bathroom? Church?
4. Do you use your cell phone while driving? Has this ever caused an accident or near accident?
5. Are there any tips you would like to add to my top ten list? What are they? Any tips you disagree with?

CHAPTER 8

D.Riving W.Hile D.Istracted

Intexticated:

Distracted by the act of texting to such a degree that one seems intoxicated.

— *Anonymous*

We all know the tell-tale signs.... a hand over the right ear of the driver in front of us, someone driving 50 miles per hour on the Interstate. Or, the slow "lane drift" as the driver in front or beside you slowly creeps into your lane and then corrects his lane tracking before he does it all over again. The "mobile" phone is no misnomer. As many as 100 million U.S. drivers admit to talking or texting while driving.[45] As many as 91 percent said they talk on their cell phone while driving and a surprisingly 50 percent confess to texting while operating a motor vehicle.[46]

The debate on cell phone use while driving comes down to our ability as humans to multitask. Can we hold conversations, check e-mails, surf the Internet, or text a friend while operating a motor vehicle? Many of us think we can but what does the data say? The National Safety Council (NSC), is a non-profit, non-governmental public service organization, whose mission is to "protect life and promote health" in the United States.[47]

The NSC has taken a careful look at whether humans can operate motor vehicles safely while using their cell phones. In a brief report entitled, "The Great Multitasking Lie," I think you know where this is going, the people at NSC lay to rest the idea that we can operate 2,000 pound-plus motor vehicles without placing ourselves and others at risk. I call it "The Great Driving While Distracted Disconnect." The majority of us have acknowledged that talking and texting while driving are two of the most dangerous things we can do behind the wheel, yet 81% of drivers admit to talking or making a phone call while driving.[48]

The fine folks at NSC are doing their best to debunk the multitasking lie that we can operate a motor vehicle safely while using our cell phone. They focus their attention on four myths about multitasking that they feel "blinds" the driving public to the dangers of cell phone use while driving.

The first myth they debunk is that drivers can multitask. In fact, the very idea that humans can multitask is shot down as a common misconception. Driving a car and using a cell phone, argues NSC, are both thinking tasks that require the involvement of many different areas of our brain. We can't do both things simultaneously, so our brain attempts to switch back and forth between each of the activities. So, any even momentary focus on our cell phone conversation comes at the expense of lack of attention to our driving task.

The NSC uses the example of walking and chewing gum to make their point. The common thinking goes, if we can walk and chew gum at the same time, we should be able to use our cell phone while driving. This analogy, however, is a poor one. Walking is a thinking task but chewing gum is a non-thinking task.

This reminds me of a funny story about my daughter Chloe' when she was a child—maybe six or seven years old. Her mother warned her that it probably wasn't a good idea to read a book while taking our nightly walk. But, as kids will do, she insisted and promptly tripped on the curb and skinned her knee—so much for multitasking.

A second myth is that talking to someone on your cell phone while driving is no different than talking to a passenger in the car. Wrong again. The NSC cites a study out of the University of Utah that found that drivers talking on their cell phone are "more oblivious" to constantly changing traffic conditions because the person on the other end of "the line" (old habits die hard) have no idea of the current traffic conditions currently being encountered.

On the other hand, a passenger is experiencing the same road conditions as the driver and acts as an "extra set of eyes and ears" regarding the driving situation. A conscientious passenger may quit talking when the driving situation warrants greater concentration or even provide advice or warnings about various traffic developments. The conversant on the other end of the line is blissfully unaware of any such developments and can only act as a distraction to the driver.

A third myth debunked by NSC is that "hands-free" devices will solve any problems created by driver inattention while using their cell phone. Oh, if this were only the case. Whether its hand-held or hands-free the conversation remains a distraction because your brain is still attempting to deal with two thinking tasks (driving and talking) simultaneously. To support their contention, the NSC cites a study out of Carnegie Mellon University, that found activity in your brain's parietal lobe "that processes movement of usual images and is important for safe driving, decreases by as much as 37% when listening to language..."[49] Referred to as "inattention blindness," drivers talking on their cell phone miss as much as 50% of their driving landscape including stop signs, pedestrians, or on-coming traffic.

The fourth myth debunked by NSC is a big one, but still kind of a lame excuse by cell phone drivers. The excuse goes something like this, "well, I may have lost some reaction time while talking on my phone, but it's better than drunk driving." Sad, I know, but astonishingly not true. A study at the University of Utah found that drivers using their cell phone actually had slower reaction times than drivers who were legally drunk (.08 blood-alcohol content).

Texting while driving is equivalent to drinking four beers before getting behind the wheel.[50] That's hard to believe, our friend who had a few too many drinks at Applebee's after work is less of a menace than those of us who choose to check on "what's for dinner" on our drive home from work.

Let me tell you a short story about an experiment conducted for Car and Driver Magazine that addressed this very issue of texting and driving versus drinking and driving.[51]

I like this experiment because it was done under as realistic circumstances as possible. The premise was simple. A red light was mounted on the top of the dashboard and was used to represent the brake lights of a car in front of you. Car & Driver rented the taxiway of the Oscoda—Wurtsmith Airport in Oscoda, Michigan. The study's two subjects included Jordan Brown, a 22 year old (at the time of the test) Web intern at Car & Driver who would use his iPhone and represented younger drivers.

His fellow subject, representing us oldsters, was Eddie Alterman, 37 (still a kid in my book). Eddie would use his Samsung Alias. Both would be driving the same Honda Pilot. The drivers were instructed to hit the brakes as soon as they saw the red light mounted on the dashboard light up. Michael Austin, the author of the article that described the experiment's results would be riding shotgun and would switch the trigger to light the red dashboard light, and record the drivers' performance. With each test drive, the red light would be switched on at intermittent intervals and the driver's response time would be logged.

The initial test drive recorded each driver's reaction time at 35 and 70 mph without any cell phone use. Next, the drivers were asked to stop the car when the red light flashed while reading a text message (quotes from the movie Caddy Shack). The next test drive had the drivers texting the same Caddy Shack quotes at 35 and 70 mph as well.

Now, here's where it gets interesting. The drivers left their vehicle and imbibed in several cocktails—screwdrivers to be more precise (a mixture of vodka and OJ). The two drivers nearly completed a fifth of Smirnoff Vodka and both easily reached the .08 blood-alcohol content level needed to reach intoxication as defined by the powers that be.

The drivers then returned to the driver's seat and their reaction times were tested with the dashboard red light again at both 35 and 70 mph. The table below tells the story best.

35MPH

Average Reaction Times & Distance Traveled

	Reaction Time (sec.)		Extra Distance Traveled (feet)	
	Brown	Alterman	Brown	Alterman
Baseline	0.45	0.57		
Reading a text	0.57	1.44	6	45
Texting	0.52	1.36	4	41
Impaired	0.46	0.64	1	7

70MPH

Average Reaction Times & Distance Traveled

	Reaction Time (sec.)		Extra Distance Traveled (feet)	
	Brown	Alterman	Brown	Alterman
Baseline	0.39	0.56		
Reading a text	0.50	0.91	11	36
Texting	0.48	1.24	9	70
Impaired	0.50	0.60	11	4

Source: Michael Austin, "Texting While Driving: How dangerous is it?", Car & Driver, June 2009, http://v./ww.caranddriver.ccnn/features/texting -while -driving-how-dangerous-is it/

Standing in for the youngsters, intern Jordan Brown's reaction time in seconds increased from .45 with no distractions to .57 at 35 mph while reading a text and nearly returned to his baseline reaction time while drunk on screwdrivers. At 70 mph, Brown's baseline reaction time was .39 seconds and was .50 while reading texts and .48 while typing texts. His reaction time at 70 mph was about the same when he was sauced as when he was reading or writing texts. Reaction time is fine and dandy, however, when the rubber hits the road (so to speak) what really counts is the extra distance traveledp because of the delayed reaction time caused by texting.

At 35 mph, Jordan traveled as much as 21 feet extra (the table on the previous page displays the average distance traveled before hitting the brakes) when reading a text and 16 feet further when texting compared to 7 feet when inebriated. At 70 mph, the results are even scarier. At 70 mph, you are covering 103 feet each second. So, while Jordan was reading a text, he traveled 30 more feet than he did compared to his baseline reaction time, but only 15 feet further than his fastest reaction time when he was drunk.

But let's not forget Eddie Alterman representing us age-challenged drivers. Eddie's baseline reaction time at 35 mph (.57) mushroomed to 1.44 seconds while reading a text. His texting time wasn't much better, 1.36 seconds. As Austin notes, this means Eddie traveled an extra 45 and 41 feet before slamming on the brakes while reading a text and texting. His reaction time while sauced was pretty close to his baseline reaction time (.64 vs. .57). This translates into traveling seven extra feet before hitting the brakes when intoxicated. Going faster can only make things worse. While reading a text Eddie's reaction time slowed to .91, writing a text slowed reaction time to 1.24 seconds. His intoxicated reaction time, however, was only slightly elevated (.60 vs. a baseline of .56).

The above does not paint a very pretty picture of a human's ability to operate a motor vehicle while using a cell phone. Both drivers traveled considerable distances when attempting to stop when operating a cell phone. Alterman's texting time at 70 mph means that the car traveled 319 feet (a football field is 300 feet) before he hit the brake after seeing the red light. Remarkably, both drivers have better reaction times when drunk compared to when reading or sending texts (they were roughly the same for the younger Brown at 70 mph).

Not to beat a dead horse, but after reading the above you might be thinking, "those are just a couple examples of the dangers of texting and driving. I'm still not convinced." Let me share with you one more test of the impact of cell phone use on driving and conclude with a brief summary of much of all the research done to date about cell phone use and driving.

Researchers David Strayer and Frank Drews of the University of Utah studied the impact of hands-free cell phone use on driving.[52] Instead of an abandoned airport runway, the two studied driver performance while using a hands-free cell phone while operating a driving simulator. All of the four studies were designed to test what the researchers referred to as the "inattention-blindness" (IB) hypothesis. The IB basically states that when a driver talks on a cell phone while driving his attention is diverted from processing driving-relevant information required to operate a motor vehicle safely.

In laymen's terms, it's hard to drive safely when you're not paying attention. Like I mentioned earlier in my discussion of the NSC, the current authors felt that hands-free conversations were no safer than hand-held cell phone conversations. Again, both require thinking (at least for most conversations) and so our brain must jump back and forth between tasks creating an opportunity for driving mishaps.

In the first study, subjects driving in a state-of-the-art driving simulator were twice as likely to recognize roadway signs when just driving compared to holding a conversation on a hands-free device mounted inside the driving simulator. In a second study, researchers placed 30 objects that were likely to be found while driving (pedestrians, stop signs, cars, billboards, etc.) along the route taken by the driving simulator. Again, drivers who were involved in only a single task (driving only) were more likely to recognize objects than those who were driving while talking on the handsfree device.

The result of both studies 1 and 2 came to the same conclusion; cell phone conversations divert driver's attention away from the driving task. Interrupting what I am sure are the numerous scintillating conversations we all have while talking on our cell phone and driving.

Even brain activity is stunted when talking and driving. A third study found that brain activity while attempting to follow a lead-car on a multiple lane highway was greatly impaired when talking on a hands-free cell phone. The important implication of this study is that the reduced brain activity (trying to do two things at once) will lead to slower reaction times when a driver's attention is distracted by a cell phone conversation.

The final study may be my favorite. The researchers investigated the impact of finding a rest stop exit approximately 8 miles down the multilane highway. The difference was that in one situation the driver was talking on a cell phone while in the other they were talking to a friend in the seat next to them. It was hypothesized that a difference would exist because a passenger is likely to adjust their conversation to match the changing driving task and might even help with navigating and pointing out potential hazards.

As hypothesized, 88% of the drivers who were talking to a friend successfully navigated the task and found the rest stop. Only 50 percent of the drivers talking on the cell phone were able to do so. Passengers were more likely to help the driver navigate and avoid road hazards and reminded them to stop. This, of course, is not possible when your only connection to the other person is wireless. Simply put, talking on a cell phone, hands-free or hand-held, interrupts the timely processing of information relevant to the driving task.

One last study I want to share with you is based upon a summary of many of the studies that have been done that have examined the impact of cell phone use on driving.[53] As a researcher myself, I place a lot of stock in such summaries because they aren't based on a single study that could be flawed, but try to generate a consensus from the research done in a given area. Researchers William Horrey and Christopher Wickens summarized twenty-three studies that examined the impact of cell phone use on driving.

Their results are significant and somewhat surprising. The meat of their findings is: (1) using cell phones while driving decreased driver performance. This decrease was biggest in reaction time (essential in avoiding accidents and less so for lane tracking—drifting in and out of one's lane.) (2) Hands-free devices were no better than hand-held when it comes to reaction time and lane drifting. This suggests that conversations are a cognitive (thinking of two things at once) and not manual difficulties of handling a hand-held device. (3) Surprisingly, conversations with passengers, the authors conclude, were just as likely to decrease driver performance as cell phone conversations.

It appears that after a careful look at the existing research, it seems safe to conclude that any type of cell phone use (hand-held or hands-free) while driving impairs driving performance. And, the cost of continuing to use our cell phones while driving is astoundingly high. The US Department of Transportation reports that cell phone use while driving causes approximately 500,000 injuries and claims 6,000 lives each year.[54] The NSC estimates that 21 percent of all car crashes, 1.2 million total, involve talking on hands-free or hand-held cell phones.

An additional 6 percent of all car crashes, argues the NSC, were caused by texting and driving. That's an additional 341,000 crashes in 2013. You can do the math, in 2013, 27% of all car crashes were due to cell phone use while driving. Drivers using a cell phone while driving are four times more likely to be involved in a car crash. Let's estimate that each car crash causes an estimated $9,100 in property damage. If you multiply the estimated 1.2 million car crashes that are the result of cell phone use while driving by $9,100 it ends up costing all of us a lot of money, about $9 billion and change.

But the financial cost is nothing compared to the 6,000 people who lost their life last year because of cell phone use while driving. That number only really hits home if you have lost a loved one or been injured by a driver distracted by his cell phone. Oprah's story of Shelley and Daren Forney from Fort Collins, CO makes a powerful point about the dangers of using a cell phone while driving.

The pair lost their nine year old daughter Erica 15 feet from their front door when she was struck and killed while driving her bicycle by a distracted driver talking on his/her cell phone. Any parent can relate to the heartache of such a senseless death. And, that it didn't have to happen only makes it worse. Oprah's message: "Dnt Txt N Drv."[55]

Although each of us are responsible for the decisions we make, partial responsibility for the current cell phone while driving imbroglio needs to rest with the cell phone industry itself. From its earliest days the cell phone industry has touted the cell phone as something to be used while driving.

This blatant disregard for public safety has not gone unnoticed.[56] The first lawsuit that targeted cell phone manufacturers and carriers occurred in 2009. The daughter of a woman killed by a 20 year old young man while he was driving and talking on his cell phone filed a wrongful death law suit in Oklahoma. The daughter sued both Sprint Nextel and Samsung for not sufficiently warning people of the dangers of using a cell phone while driving. The accused driver admitted to being distracted while talking on his Samsung cell phone which caused him to run a red-light (see studies mentioned earlier) and strike and kill Linda Doyle while traveling at 45 mph.

Sprint, of course, argues that sufficient warning was given but the young man claims not to have been aware of any such warnings. Yes, the young man should have been aware of the dangers of cell phone use and driving but, like the tobacco companies, the cell phone industry should launch a more aggressive public service campaign that addresses the dangers of cell phone use while driving. Given the embedded nature of our cell phone use, however, I don't believe it would do much good.

Food for Thought

1. Do you use your cell phone when driving a car? Text?
2. Have you had a close call when driving because of your cell phone use? What happened?
3. Do you know anyone who was in an accident caused by cell phone use while driving?
4. Do "Hands-Free" devices make driving while using your smartphone safer?
5. Can humans multitask? Why or why not?

CHAPTER 9

Making the Grade(s)

Multitasking:
The practice of attempting to do two or more things at one time.

Bottleneck:
A point of blockage in a system that occurs when multiple tasks arrive at the same time and overwhelm the system such that it can't adequately process them. The blockage brought about by the bottleneck often creates a queue and requires more time to finish the tasks at hand.[57]

Seventy percent of college professors do it. I can't imagine the bedlam for the thirty percent that don't. I am talking about classroom policies regarding technology use. Being well versed in the distracting nature of cell phones and laptops, my classroom policy on technology use is simple: off and out of sight. Recall, in chapter six where we talked about research that found that even the mere presence of a cell phone can be distracting. They don't even have to be on. I love technology and all the things that can be accomplished with it, but it interferes with learning in the classroom and this chapter provides evidence to support such a claim.

Despite my very clear policy on technology use in the classroom, you guessed it; I still have problems with it as I am sure every other college professor in the world does. I will get a few ringing cell phones, often stylized, but the biggest problem is texting. I will share some interesting survey statistics with you later that tell us that pretty much everybody is texting in class at one time or another. The head facing down with eyes focused on their lap is a sure sign that my students are not pondering the nuances of cluster sampling but are most likely making lunch plans with their friends. They could be checking sports scores or Instagram but it's mostly texting.

And, as we found out in chapter two, many students can't help being distracted by their cell phones because they are addicted. What else could explain the willingness of a student to continue to use his or her cell phone after getting repeated dirty looks from the professor, being asked to put it away in front of classmates, and even warned of being asked to leave class? Such warnings are repeated daily in college classrooms around the world.

So, the $64,000.00 question is: Does the student use of cell phones or other technology in and outside of class impact their academic performance? It's probably best to start out by discussing the capabilities of the human brain. When someone is asked what they are doing when they are doing homework on their iPad, checking their cell phones periodically, and surfing the web on their laptop, they usually reply, "I am multitasking." In a very broad sense they are correct, they are doing multiple things at the same time but not necessarily simultaneously.

The sad truth, however, is that humans can't multitask. The concept of multitasking began with computers. Computers do have the ability to multitask. A computer can run a number of different applications at the same time without compromising its performance. Humans cannot. A long line of research studies has proven that performance suffers when we try to do more than one thing at a time.

They call it a "cognitive bottleneck." It's the point where all the compelling information we are attempting to process at once backs up at the narrow neck of our brain's computing (pardon the pun) capacity. Scads of research over the years has supported the existence of such a bottleneck. Humans are incapable of true multitasking. When we are doing three or four things at once, we are not multitasking but "task switching"— rapidly switching back and forth from one task to the other.

The problem with task switching is that it leads to lower comprehension (if you were in class on your laptop) and takes longer to complete the desired tasks. It's like my grandmother used to say, "concentrate and you'll be done sooner" or "turn off the TV (or radio) and finish your work then you can have some fun." It takes longer to complete tasks because you lose time every time you switch from one task to another. Research suggests multitaskers may reduce their productivity by an astounding 40 percent when they switch back and forth between tasks.[58]

Believe it or not, you will do better (and finish sooner) if you were to do each task serially. One's attention must be divided between each of the desired tasks, and since we all may deal with limited cognitive capacity, the performance on one task gets in the way of completing the other tasks.

Having a cell phone in class increases the likelihood of multitasking (really task switching) considerably, leading to a lower comprehension of class lectures or discussions. One way to explain multitasking's negative effect on classroom learning is "Load Theory." Our ability to work on more than one task at a time depends on how much working memory resources are available. Social technologies like Facebook or texting require a lot of working memory resources that crowd out my brilliant lecture on the marketing research process (it's one of my favorites).[59]

Incredibly, research tells us that 73 percent of college students said they were not able to study without some type of technology. Thirty-eight percent said they couldn't last ten minutes without checking their cell phone or laptop. Truth is students become distracted by their cell phones in less than six minutes after beginning studying. Even more astounding than the above statistics is research that has found that multitasking causes a drop in your IQ of 10 points (I don't have that much to spare) which is the equivalent of going a night without sleep.[60] I call this the "Gomer Pyle" effect of multitasking.

So, are all my beautifully crafted lectures on cell phones and learning falling on deaf ears or being stuck in a cognitive bottleneck? Earlier in Chapter seven on cell phone etiquette, I quoted some interesting statistics that might help answer this question. Recall that 44 percent of college students said it was appropriate to have your cell phone on your desk, 42 percent said it was okay to text during class, 37 percent felt fine with surfing the web during class and 35 percent thought it was kosher to send e-mails while in class. Eight percent thought it was fine to even make calls.

And, my daughter who just completed her freshman year of college confirms this. In her large lecture classes she said it looks like the encore at a Soulja Boy concert with nearly everybody fiddling with their phone during class. I wondered out loud when we had this discussion if students are going to so blatantly disregard the lectures in such classes that they might just as well be taught online.

So, what do the polls say? Have students really become so enamored (addicted?) that their school life has become a distraction from their cell phone? In a large sample of 777 college students, University of Nebraska—Lincoln researcher, Barney McCoy, found that nearly one-third of all students used a digital device (mostly cell phones but lap tops too) more than 11 times during class for non-class related topics (texting a friend, posting to Instagram, checking last night's scores, etc.). With that kind of task switching I am surprised that any subject matter sticks. More than 90 percent of students polled reported that they use some type of digital device during class time. Of these, 86 percent texted, two-thirds visited a social networking site and/or sent an e-mail, over one-third surfed the web and nearly eighty percent checked the time.

What's more confounding is that the students themselves felt that using digital devices during class was distracting. Thirty-seven percent said it wasn't a distraction but about 62 percent said it was a source of distraction. Fifty-four percent of students feel that professors should have some type of policy regarding technology use in the classroom but only nine percent feel it should be banned completely.[61] There appears to be a real disconnect between student usage of their cell phones and attitudes about their use within the classroom. In one poll, eighty percent of students say they have texted in class yet many of those same students felt it is inappropriate to do so.[62] As one eminent psychologist explained, it is simply a matter of self-control. Students (and adults at work as well) simply can't control their behavior when it comes to their cell phones. The fruit is simply too sweet to resist.

So, you might be asking, "why should I care about all this?" The answer to this question is an easy one. Considerable research has found that using technology in the classroom or while studying (or at work) will likely lower your academic performance—your GPA will be lower. You might say, "He's making this up just to get me to put down my cell phone" or essentially, "prove it."

Let me take a stab at "proving it." The real guru in the debate regarding the impact of technology on academic performance is Reynol Junco a professor at Iowa State University. He has written three books on technology in the classroom and countless articles about technology and learning. In a recent study, Professor Junco surveyed 1,649 undergraduate students and asked them how much time they spent on Facebook and the time they spent multitasking while on Facebook (studying while on Facebook).[63]

Study results suggest that the more time Freshman spent with Facebook led to lower grades. Professor Junco reasoned that Facebook helps freshman adjust to their new surroundings. It appears, however, that this time spent on Facebook has a negative impact on their grades. Multitasking with Facebook while studying was found to lead to lower GPA for all underclassmen with the exception of seniors. This later finding provides solid support that multitasking interferes with our ability to process information effectively. Not to be Facebook bashing, but a study of 102 graduate students found that multitasking with Facebook led not only to lower GPAs but fewer hours studying in general compared to new users.[64]

Two fascinating experiments seem to be telling us the same thing. In the first experiment, students were placed in one of four experimental conditions. Students were asked to either use Facebook, send texts, use instant messaging or e-mail during a 20 minute video-taped lecture. The control groups were simply asked to watch the video without any distractions. Students who used Facebook scored lower on tests of lecture material than control subjects who took notes using the old fashioned paper and pencil method.[65]

In another experiment student subjects watched a 30-minute video lecture while being sent text messages by the people running the experiment. Students were placed into one of three groups:

Group 1. *0-7 text messages received during lecture (low group).*

Group 2. *8-15 text messages received (moderate group).*

Group 3. *16 or more text messages received (high group).*

After the experiment was completed all students took a test on the content of the video. The group receiving the most text messages (high group) scored an entire letter grade lower than the group receiving the fewest number of texts. What can we conclude from the above studies? We can conclude that multitasking can reduce academic performance. Distracting ourselves with technology, whether in class or while studying, can act as an impediment to student learning.

In a survey of 536 undergrads, researchers found that cell phone use negatively impacted actual (not self-reported) GPA. The researchers measured cell phone use in total minutes inside and outside of the classroom and warned students and educators alike about the potential dangers of heavy student cell phone use. No doubt, cell phones were used during study time as well as during class which interfered with the learning of study materials.[66]

Another study found that social networking sites like Facebook, Twitter, and LinkedIn can have particularly disastrous effects on student learning. In an international sample of 406 college students, researchers found that multitasking with social networking sites while studying led to lower GPAs for American Students only. This is a particularly worrisome trend since college students spend so much time on social networking sites.[67]

A study published in the College Student Journal found that students who texted more (a similar social motive to visiting SNS) have lower GPAs. The authors concluded that those students who sent fewer texts are less distracted or preoccupied with their phones than those who text more frequently and can better digest and organize class material and reflect on that material throughout the day.[68]

In sum, we are humans and not computers. When we attempt to do more than one thing at a time something has to give. I always wonder why it has to be student learning that suffers and not time on our cell phones or other technology? An easy answer might be that we are in love with our cell phones that, with their constant beeping, caterwauling, vibrations, and whistles are like the petulant (spoiled) child who will not behave until he or she gets what they want. The desire of our cell phone is to be constantly touched and attended to. Cell phones demand our attention, but, and pardon my parenting metaphor, if we let them "cry it out" we will all get a better night's sleep.

Food for Thought

1. Do you use your cell phone during class or at work? When? Why?
2. Have others' cell phone use in class or at work distracted you? Did you say anything?
3. Do you use other technologies when you're working or studying?
4. Do you consider yourself a multitasker? Do you feel this helps you be more productive?
5. Have you ever been reprimanded by your teacher or boss for using your cell phone or other technology when you shouldn't have been?

CHAPTER 10

Smartphone Smack Down: Going Off the Grid (Sometimes)

Self—Control (n): The ability to control your thoughts desires, and behavior.

"I am indeed a king, because I know how to rule myself"
— Pietro Aretino

The Paradox of Cell Phones

Cell phone use is a good example of the paradox of technology. The use of the modern smartphone can be both liberating and enslaving at the same time. You are the master of your domain when you have your smartphone at your disposal. If it's a slow day you may even make a call, but more likely you will send a text, post to Instagram or Facebook, take a few pictures, check e-mails, send a tweet, check the time or the sports scores, see how many steps you've taken since lunch or send a constant stream of Snapchat pictures to various and sundry others. You get the picture; the world is our oyster when we have our smartphones at the ready.

On the other hand, however, we can become slaves to our smartphones as well. Only 87 likes to my last post—no one loves me. He hasn't opened my Snapchat yet. Can't keep up with the conversation on "Group Me"? My frenemies seem to be having a better time on Facebook than I am having. It's nearly 11:30 p.m. but I still need to answer the e-mail from my neurotic boss or co-worker.

And, I will watch only one more cat playing the piano video before I go to bed, but I better leave my phone on and next to my bed in case anything important happens while I attempt to get some sleep despite the constant cacophony coming from my smartphone.

For both good and bad (that's why you've read this far into my book, or did you skip ahead?), cell phones are an inextricable part of our daily lives. For many of us they have become the driver and we are mere passengers in our own life story. We all sense it—something isn't right. We must be vigilant to avoid reaching the "tipping point" where our cell phone use crosses the line from a helpful tool to one that enslaves us and robs us of all the great "offline" experiences waiting for us if we take a few minutes and look up from our screens.

The good news is, you can do it. You can find your digital "sweet spot." That's the place where you call the shots instead of your smartphone. Like I have said hundreds of times about money, smartphones are poor masters but good servants. It is really nothing more than exercising a little self-control when it comes to your smartphone. Fortunately, I have written extensively about self-control in several academic articles and my book Shiny Objects. So, let's talk a few minutes about self-control and how you can find your digital "sweet spot" regarding your smartphone use.

The Three Ingredients of Self-Control

Self-control is a subject that is really quite simple to learn but hard to do. The first ingredient is awareness. You must be aware of your smartphone habits. How much time do you spend texting, on social media, playing games, tweeting, taking pictures, sending e-mails, checking your calendar, posting to Instagram, searching music sites, shopping, or, as antiquated as it might sound, actually making calls?

What time of day and where do you participate in each of these and the myriad of other activities that can be performed on the modern smartphone? Fortunately, as I will describe in greater detail in a few pages, there are plenty of apps, yes we will use "the beast" itself against itself, like "Phone Addict" (Android) or "Moment" (iOS) that can help you figure out where you are spending your time on your smartphone.

With a greater awareness of your smartphone habits you can start to plan how you are going to cut back on your smartphone use. This is where the second ingredient to self-control comes into play. You must have specific goals as to how you plan to find your digital sweet spot. For example, if your earlier investigative work shows you are spending over three hours each day on Instagram (you choose your poison), a smart goal might be to cut back (I didn't say go cold turkey) on your visits to Instagram.

There are a number of Apps that will allow you to set time limits for a specific website or activity on your smartphone. If Instagraming is a problem at night you could take drastic measures and turn off your smartphone or program one of the parental control or monitoring Apps to make that website or App unavailable, let's say, from 10:00 p.m. to 2:00 a.m. if that's the time span when you are most actively posting.

I say start small. Pick the one biggest time sink on your smartphone and set a goal to cut your use of that App or website by half. You might have to find a way to distract yourself during the "danger zone" when your Instagram posting is the highest. I suggest using your technology against itself. Simply disable your phone from going to Instagram for that time period and find something else to do.

The third ingredient of self-control is having a plan and the strength to execute your plan to bring your smartphone use to what you feel is a more comfortable level. A plan might be to do your homework or housework/chores for the hour you disable access to a particular App or website. There is an old saying, "Idle hands are the devil's workshop." Modern translation, you get into trouble when you don't have anything to do. Take the cinnamon challenge? Clearly running out of things to do. Distract yourself with a healthy and/or productive activity. This will help reinforce that shutting down Instagram for an hour was a good idea.

These ideas may sound corny but meditating, exercising, and getting a good night sleep all can be successful in executing your plan. Self-control is a limited resource—you only have so much to go around. Getting a good night's sleep, meditating and exercising help you replenish your self-control resources so you have the strength to say "no" to another epic fail compilation on YouTube.

A last word on self-control before I share several suggestions about locating your digital sweet spot. There's really only two ways for you to change your behavior: Behavioral and environmental programming. Sounds like heavy stuff but it's really not, nothing more than Psychology 101. Behavioral programming has to do with setting up a program to reward behaviors you want to continue or punish behaviors you want to extinguish.

It's simply a matter of the carrot or the stick. Rewards for desired behaviors could include self-praise "Good job Jim!" or conjuring up a pleasurable mental image (getting an "A" or a promotion at work) because of cutting back on social media. Or, a nice meal out or shopping trip could be more tangible enticements to accomplish your goals. The stick (punishments) could be self-criticism or the conjuring of negative mental images (failing a class or being passed over for a promotion at work) when you don't accomplish your goals. You could also take away things you like (movie binging) if you don't successfully cut back on your visits to YouTube.

If you go the carrot or stick route I suggest you get your spouse or friends involved by using a commitment contract. A commitment contract is simply a written document that clearly states what you hope to accomplish, how you are going to do it, by when, and what the role of your co-signer will be. Are you asking your friend or spouse to call you out when you pull out your phone between 10:00 p.m. and midnight? Or, are they going to be expected to monitor your cell phone use by checking your monitoring app and acting as the judge, jury, and executioner if you do not reach your goal or aren't making adequate progress towards it as pre-determined? Getting others involved, if the contract is well spelled out, is a great way to stay the course.

When I want to change a behavior I always first consider environmental programming which involves designing your personal environment in such a way that accomplishing your goals become easier. For me, on a non—cell phone related note, this means not eating at buffets because I always eat too much when I do. Unlike my wife, who can go to a buffet and eat a reasonable amount. I don't know if it's a "guy thing" or just me, but I just can't do it. So, to avoid failing I simply avoid buffets—problem solved.

I have always lived by the axiom that "it is easier to avoid temptation than it is to resist it." When given a choice, at least half the time most of us will give in to temptation. So, don't make yourself make choices. Program your environment so you don't have to. One simple example, if your smartphone is on and in your pocket, on your desk, or even in your backseat you are going to leap for it when it buzzes, just like Pavlov's dogs when they heard the dinner bell. Remove temptation by turning your phone off and putting it in the trunk. Sounds drastic but it works. If your smartphone is off and not in your bedroom, your spouse or romantic partner will appreciate it and you will get a good night sleep as well. Other benefits of keeping your cell phone out of your bedroom are up to you.

Smarthone Smack Down Tips

My initial inclination was to label this section "Digital Detox" but I think that's a bit unrealistic and not nearly as effective as cutting back on your everyday use of your smartphone. With a digital detox you go off the digital grid for a certain period of time. This can be very relaxing and an opportunity to reconnect with others and re-evaluate your relationship with technology. The problem is once the detox period is over the first thing you do is reach for your smartphone and the race is back on.

This is why I have entitled this section, "Smartphone Smack Down Tips." What I share below are tips I have used or found that allow you to cut back where you feel you need to while staying on the grid. Again, it's about finding your digital sweet spot where you are still plugged in but you have carved out time for the things that really matter like yourself, your friends, family, and co-workers, and issues larger than yourself (religion/spiritual activities, charity work or other good causes).

The "Big three" as I call them (you, your relationships, and community) are the real bedrocks of living a happy and meaningful life. They are also the things that suffer when our lives get out of balance. So, let's talk about a few things you can do to keep your smartphone use in check. One warning, with the ever-changing nature of technology, the Apps I refer to below may be obsolete by the time this book is published but I am comfortable that ten new and improved Apps will have been created to take their place.

Five Tips For Finding Your Digital Sweet Spot

1. **No smartphones while driving.** This is by far the easiest tip to implement and also the most important. Simply toss (place gently) your cell phone in your trunk before you leave. You won't see it (remember, even their mere presence is distracting) or hear it and you will have a greatly reduced (about 40%) chance of having a car accident. Don't become one of the legion of thousands who have died or been killed by someone using their cell phone while driving. Please refer to chapter eight for the damage wrought by drivers using cell phones and the common myths surrounding our ability to maneuver a 2,500 pound vehicle while texting. I have found the

quiet car time before work has allowed me to plan my day and after work I have a chance to decompress before I hit the casa. Trust me, my wife and kids appreciate a decompressed husband and father.

2. **Set cell phone free zones and times.** Cell phones should be forbidden in certain places at home and work. First and foremost, no cell phones in the bedroom. Spend this time better by reconnecting with your spouse or simply slowing down before you hit the sack. Humans need to avoid the LED lights from cell phones, laptops, and other electronic devices for at least a half hour before going to bed.

    The dinner table should also be a cell phone free zone. Everyone needs to leave their cell phone out of sight and hearing distance. I bought a funny little cell phone "prison" where everybody must place their cell phone in it and then you can set the amount of time before the warden can "free" them.

    At work, I suggest you designate two or three times (at the most) where you allow yourself to check your smartphone for any messages, updates, or other goodies that might be waiting your attention. The remainder of the time your phone should be off and out of sight. You will be shocked at how much more productive you are when you're not distracted by your smartphone. I stopped counting how many times I stopped while writing this book to check e-mails because I could see the e-mail icon on my computer screen. But I can say that my cell phone has not been a distraction during my writing of this book (self-praise as mentioned above).

3. **"Hair of the Dog."** I call this "Hair of the Dog" because I am pitting technology against technology. I won't list all of the apps here that you can use to monitor and control your smartphone use but let's talk about a few. Moment is an iOS App that can tell you how many times you've handle your iPhone in a given day and where you've been and how much time you've spent on each activity. You can also set time limits from between five minutes and six hours for any particularly distraction or time consuming activity that you perform on your smartphone.

Phone Addict is the equivalent to Moment for Android users. It tracks the time you spend on your phone (or tablet) over a long period of time as well as daily use. An interesting feature is that public shaming can be programmed into this app. You can share with your friends or accountability partner how much time you're spending on social media. This feature could be used as a high-tech component of a commitment contract you signed with your spouse, friends, or family members to help you cut back on your cell phone time. Rescue Time tracks and reports on much time you've spent on certain websites and apps and creates a daily dashboard to shame you with. It can also block websites. If social media is a real problem, Anti—Social (great name) will block Twitter, Facebook, Pinterest, and Instagram for you. This sounds a little rough but it just might be what the doctor ordered.

If you're struggling with controlling your e-mail try unroll. me or the app Mailbox to cut out the spam so you only get what you want and or need. I hope these apps work better than my spam filter at work that continues to allow a lot of junk into my inbox. We both live and die by technology.

4. **Go the "Dumb—phone" route.** When it comes down to it, all we really need is to be able to receive and send calls and texts. Sure e-mail is nice. And so is catching up on social media, but the dumb-phone at least keeps us safe (the long-forgotten original purpose for cell phones) and able to keep in touch with those we need to. Or, as one reporter suggests, you could carry a nophone. It is essentially a piece of plastic (could be wood) that looks like a cell phone but is just there to comfort someone if they are experiencing withdrawals from their cell phone. It's the same as pulling out a stick of gum when you're trying to cut back on your smoking.

5. **"Just Do It."** All of the above suggestions will come to naught if you have not totally committed yourself to the case. You must convince yourself that curbing your smartphone is critical to your happiness before you embark on this journey. If not, you are doomed to fail. I liken cutting back on your smartphone use while the rest of the world goes on its merry way to a salmon swimming upstream. You will take some flack and may even miss out on a few great cat YouTube videos and Instagram posts but hopefully a deeper sense of relaxation, greater piece of mind, deeper relationships, and a enlarged sense of community will more than make up for anything you might miss when you're off grid.

Adbusters, who sponsors "Digital Detox Week," offers several suggestions to deepen your resolve to curb your smartphone dependence. The first suggests taking a "Zen Moment." When you wake up in the morning stare into your blank smartphone screen for a minute and ponder your reflection in the still dark screen. What role do you want this latest piece of technology to play in your life? Adbusters also suggests that you slow down and provides a link to a 60-second animated video about the hectic pace of modern life. The video should spark conversations on how living life at a break-neck speed comes at a great cost to you (mentally and physically), to your relationships, and your ability to plug into larger causes.[69]

Create a list of the costs of being connected and the benefits that could accrue from cutting back and ponder it. Take walks with your spouse and/or friends (without your smartphones) and discuss your attachment to your smartphone. For you brave souls, cleanse yourself by detoxing (total abstinence from your cell phone) for a day, evening, or even a weekend. This off grid time will give you the opportunity to think deeply about your technology use. Don't expect it to be easy. New habits can take a while to form. And, if you are deeply attached, or even addicted, to your smartphone, you will likely suffer withdrawal symptoms (irritability, anxiety, panic, restlessness, etc.) similar to people kicking substance abuse disorders.

These symptoms and others, including phantom vibrations, were experienced by a group of 200 college students when they attempted to kick the media habit (no cell phones, TV, laptops, etc.) for one day. The results were not pretty. The word "addiction" was brought up a lot when participants recounted their experiences. Many found excuses to drop out long before the

24 hours was up. They talked about feeling disconnected from friends and family. The experience was an eye-opening one for all and prompted much soul searching amongst the participants.[70]

Trading a Meaningful Life For Monetary Pleasures

In one of my favorite cell phone related stories, a man was on a whale watching tour off the coast of Redondo Beach, California, blissfully engrossed with his cell phone when completely unaware of what was going on a few feet in front of him, a 52 foot, 30-50 ton giant humpback whale surfaced and meandered at the surface for some time before submerging. As if lightning never strikes twice, the same whale surfaced again, dallied for a few moments and then returned to the deep. The man engrossed with his cell phone, sitting splashing distance away from the breaching whale missed it all. How do we know this? Another boat of whale watchers caught it all on tape—no doubt on their smartphones.[71]

Don't, like this guy, trade the momentary pleasures afforded by your cell phone for all the great stuff that happens offline. As made abundantly clear in the preceding chapters of this book, without a clear policy on smartphones and other technologies we risk missing the boat, or the whale in this story.

Food for Thought

1. Have you found your digital "sweet spot"? If no, what are your plans to do so?
2. How could you use the three ingredients of self-control to help you achieve your digital sweet spot?
3. How can you program your environment to curb your smartphone use?
4. Try an app that can help you monitor and control your smartphone use. Send me a text and let me know how it worked.
5. How can you use behavioral programming to curb your smartphone use?

ENDNOTES

Chapter 1

1. Finkel and Kruger (2012) "Is Cell Phone Use Socially Contagious?", The International Society for Human Ethology.

2. Seyyed Salman Alavi, et al. (2011), "Behavioral addiction versus substance addiction: Correspondence of psychiatric and psychological views," International Journal of Preventive Medicine, vol. 3, no. 4, pages 290-294.

3. Mark Griffiths (1999), "Internet Addiction: fact or Fiction?" *The Psychologist: Bulletin of the British Psychological Society*, 12, pages 246-250; Mark Griffiths(2000), "Does Internet and Computer "Addiction" exist? Some case study evidence," *CyberPsychology & Behavior*, no.2, pages 211-218; Joanna Brenner, "PEW Internet: Mobile" (2012); James A. Roberts and Stephen F. Pirog, III (2012), A preliminary investigation of materialism and impulsiveness as predictors of technological addictions among young adults," *Journal of Behavioral Addictions*.

4. Griffiths (2000)

5. CTIA—The Wireless Association, http://www.ctia.org/

6. http://www.phones4charity.org, accessed 5-16-2013.

7. Junco, Reynol, and Sheila R. Cotton (2012). No A 4 U: The relationship between multitasking and academic performance. *Computers & Education*, 59, 505-514; Junco, Reynol, and Gail A. Cole-Avent (2008), "An Introduction to Technologies Commonly Used by College Students," New Directions For Student Services, 124 (Winter), 3-17.

8. Wadyka, "Are You Addicted to Your Cell phone?"

9. Fiona Keating, "Got a Smartphone? You probably check Facebook fourteen times a day," MailOnline, http:// www.dailymail.co.uk/sciencetech/article-2300466/smartphone-users-check-facebook ...., accessed 3-28-2013.

10. PEW Internet: Mobile (2012)

11. Junco & Cole-Avent, 2008

12. David Glen Mick & Susan Fournier (1998), "Paradoxes of technology: Consumer cognizance, emotions, and coping strategies," Journal of Consumer research, vol. 25 (September), pages 123-143.

Chapter 2

13. "Cell phones key to teens social lives, 47% can text with eyes closed," CTIA & Harris interactive survey (2008.), http://www.marketing charts.com/interactive/cell phoneskey-to-teens-social-lives-47-can-t.., accessed 6-10-2011.

14. Ibid.

15. Roberts & Manolis—CP usage and addiction study (under review)

16. Sally Wadyka, "Are you Addicted to your phone?," http://healthyliving.msn.com/blogs/daily-apple-blogpost?post=b2ad70cf-9c33-4a8b-bd66, accessed 2/15/2013

17. Statistic Brain Research Institute, http://www.statisticbrain.com/attention-span-statistics/, accessed 6-17-2015; Lizzette Burrell, "Human attention span shortens to 8 seconds due to digital technology: 3 ways to stay focused," http://www.medicaldaily.com/human-attention-span-shortens-8seconds-due-digital-techn..., accessed 6-17-2015.

18. Grover et al.(2011), "From use to abuse: When everyday consumption behaviors morph into addictive consumption behaviours," Journal of research for Consumers, issue 19.

19. Ibid.

20. Ibid.

21. Mark Griffiths (1999), "Internet Addiction: Fact or Fiction?", *The Psychologist: Bulletin of the British Psychology Society.*

22. Mobile Device / Cell Phone Statistics, http://www.statisticbrain.com/mobile-device-cell phone-statistics/, accessed 4-5-2013.

23. Sally Wadyka—Healthy Living; Kleiner, Perkins, Caufield and Byers "Annual Internet Trends Report" (2013).

24. IDC/Facebook (2013), "Always connected: How Smartphones and Social Keep Us Engaged."

25. "Cell Phone Statistics: Updated 2012," http://www.Accuconference.com/blog/cell phone-statistics.aspx, accessed 4-5-2013.

26. Billieux et al. (2008), The role of impulsivity in actual and problematic use of the mobile phone, Applied Cognitive Psychology, 22, pages 1195-1210.

27. Keith Albow (2012), "Why cell phone addiction is now on the rehab menu," http://www.foxnews.com/ health/2012/09/21/why-mobile-phone-addic-

tion-is-now-on-reha..., accessed 2-11-2013; 66% of the population suffer from Nomophobia the fear of being without their phone," http://www.securenvy.com/blog/2012/02/16/66-of-the-population-suffer-from-nomophob..., accessed 5-13-2013.

28. A Day without media, http://withoutmedia.wordpress.com/, accessed 4-15-2013.

Chapter 4

29. The term "phubbing" was created in 2012 at Sydney University by a group of language specialists at the behest of the advertising agency McCann Melbourne as a promotional campaign for the Macquarie Dictionary. It was also part of a "stop phubbing" campaign by the same agency.

30. Items 1 and 4 have been adapted from McDaniel and Coyne's (2014) TILES scale.

Chapter 5

31. Jennifer Ludden, "Can social media break up a marriage?" All Things Considered, 11-2-2010

32. Brandom T. McDaniel and Sarah M. Coyne, "Technoference": The interference of technology in couple relationships and implications for women's personal and relational well-being, *Psychology of Popular Media Culture*, 2014.

33. Sherry Turkle, *Alone Together*, 2012

34. Andrew K. Przybylski and Netta Weinstein, Can you connect with me now? How the presence of mobile communication technology influences face-to-face conversation quality, *Journal of Social and Personal Relationships*, 2012.

35. The first two items of the cell phone conflict slate have been modified from Theiss and Solamon's (2006) Directness of Communication Scale.

Chapter 6

36. McDaniel and Coyne, 2014; James A. Roberts and Meredith David, My life has become a major distraction from my cell phone: Partner phubbing and relationship satisfaction among romantic partners, under review.

37. McDaniel and Coyne, 2014.

38. Items 1, 2, and 3 of the Partner Phubbing Scale are slight modifications of three items from McDaniel and Coyne's (2014) TILES Scale.

Chapter 7

39. Christine Rosen, "The gadget and the bad Samaritan," *Wall Street Journal*, Saturday/Sunday, October 26/27, 2013, C3.

40. Center for the Digital Future survey finds generation gap in cell phone etiquette, http://annenberg.usc.edu/news/around-usc-annenberg/center-digital-future-survey-finds-gen..., accessed 6-5-2015.

41. "Infographic: The state of smartphone etiquette," http://www.ragan.com/main/articles/infographic_the_state_of_smartphone_etiquette_47..., accessed 2-25-2015.

42. "The miss manners of cell phones," http://archive.wired.com/gadgets/wireless/news/2001/09/46448.

43. "Cell phone etiquette and dating," http://jacquelinewhitmore.com/cell phone-etiquette-and-dating/, accessed on 6-5-2015.

44. "How to use your cell phone in public," http://wikihow.com/use-your-cell phone-in-public, and "How to practice cell phone etiquette," http://www.wikihow.com/practice-cell phone-etiquette, accessed 6-5-2015. "Infographic: The state of smartphone etiquette."

Chapter 8

45. David L. Strayer & Frank A. Drews (2007), "Cell phone-induced driver distraction, Current Directions in Psychological Science, vol. 16, no. 3.

46. Pinchot et al. (2011), "How mobile technology is changing our culture," Journal of Information Systems Applied Research, 4 (1), pages 39-48.

47. www.NSC.org, accessed 6-15-2015.

48. "Cell phone & Texting Accident Statistics," http://www.edgarsnyder.com/car-accident/cell-phonr/cell phone-statistics.html, accessed 6-15-2015.

49. National Safety Council (NSC)—Multitasking Myth #3, http://www.nsc.org/safety-road/distracted_driving/pages/ddam.aspx, accessed 6-2-2015.

50. Jacob Masters, "Texting while driving Vs. drunk driving: Which is more dangerous?," http://www.bisociety.org/texting-while-driving-vs-drunk-driving-which-is-more-dangerous/, accessed 6-17-2015.

51. Texting while driving; How dangerous is it? Michael Austen— Car + Driver, June 2009.

52. David l. Strayer and frank A. Drews (2007), "Cell phone-Induced driver Distraction, Current Directions in Psychological Science, vol. 16, no. 3.

53. William J. Horrey & Christopher D. Wickens (2006), "Examining the impact of cell phone conversations on driving usinf meta-analytic techniques, 48, no. 1, 196-205.

54. "Don't text and drive," http://www.donttextdrive.com/statistics/, accessed 6-16-2015

55. Oprah Winfrey (2010), "Oprah's Message: Dnt Txt N Drive," New York Times, April 25th.

56. "First wrongful death lawsuit against cell phone manufacturer and carrier," www.filutowskilae.com/2009/12/firstwrongful-death-lawsuit-against-cell phone-man, accessed 3/6/2013.

Chapter 9

57. http://www.investopdeia.com/terms/b/bottleneck.asp, accessed 6-9-2015.

58. "Multitasking (in humans)," http://whatis.techtarget.com/ definition/multitasking-in-humans, accessed 6-8-2015.

59. Reynol Junco, 2015, "student class standing, Facebook use, and academic performance," *Journal of Applied Developmental Psychology*, vol. 36, 18-29.

60. "Multitasking (in humans)," http://whatis.techtarget.com/ definition/multitasking-in-humans, accessed 6-8-2015.

61. Julia Ryan, "Study: 80% of college students say they text in class," *The Atlantic*, October 25, 2013.

62. Alan Mozes, College students admit texting in the most inappropriate places," *Health Day*, April 15, 2015.

63. Reynol Junco, 2015, "student class standing, Facebook use, and academic performance," *Journal of Applied Developmental Psychology*, vol. 36, 18-29.

64. Paul A. Kirschner and Aryn C. Karpinski, "Facebook and Academic Performance."

65. Reynol Junco, 2015, "student class standing, Facebook use, and academic performance," *Journal of Applied Developmental Psychology*, vol. 36, 18-29.

66. Andrew Lepp, Jacob E. Barkley and Aryn C. Karpinski, 2015, The relationship between cell phone use and academic performance in a sample of US college students," *Sage Open*, Jan.-March, 1-9.

67. Aryn C. Karpinski, Paul A. Kirschner, Ipek Ozer, Jennifer A. mellott, and Pius Ochwo, 2012, "An exploration of social networking site use, multitasking, and academic performance among United States and European university stduents," *Computers in Human Behavior*.

68. Brittany A. Harmon and Toru Sato, 2011, "Cell phone use and grade point average among undergraduate university students," *College Student Journal*, 544-549.

Chapter 10

69. https://www.adbusters.org/campaigns/digitaldetox, accessed 6-10-2015.

70. "A day without media," http://wihtoutmedia.wordpress. ocm/, accessed 4-5-2013.

71. Chris Spargo, "Don't text and whale watch ..." http://dailymail.co.uk/news/article-2940183/don-t-text-whale-watchphoto-captures-..., accessed 6-11-2015.

Made in the USA
Lexington, KY
27 September 2018